To Kent & Irene
    I appreciate your
service & testimony very
much & pray our fathers
blessing will be yours
in your lives & raising
your family.

        Love
        Bishop Anderson
    Venetta & the Ward.

1988

A Regular Dad

Making Fatherhood Fun

A Regular Dad

Making Fatherhood Fun

Ron Woods

To Dad
and
To C. Ray

Preface

David, our second child and first boy, was perhaps five years old when I asked him one day what he wanted to be when he grew up. Previously, his answers had been cowboy, truck driver, or fireman. But this time he caught me by surprise when he said, "Just a regular dad—like you."

"A regular dad?" What was that? Is that what I was? What had happened to my hero status in David's eyes? It took a moment, but I understood that this answer wasn't an insult to my fragile male ego; it was a compliment. What David was saying was that he wanted to be like me. "Just a regular dad" was, therefore, a nice thing to be called, after all.

As I've thought about that experience since, it's been a reminder to me of something very basic about child-rearing:

CHILDREN MODEL THEMSELVES AFTER THEIR PARENTS, ESPECIALLY THE SAME-SEX PARENT.

Of course there are other influences: friends, teachers, siblings, TV, and society in general, but, especially in the early years, dad plays a key role in the development of a boy. That's what David's answer really meant: that I was his role model. What a responsibility!

If dad is a role model for his sons, and a girl models herself after her mom, what role does dad play in the life of his daughters? Well, for one thing, many psychologists feel that a woman's ability to relate to her husband in a marriage is largely dependent on the relationship she had in her youth with her dad. Another big responsibility!

It appears, then, that a dad has a pretty important role to play in the life of his children of either sex, certainly much more than the mere providing of material support.

None of this, of course, lessens the role of a mother in the life of her children, be they boys or girls. It's just that this is a book about dads, and we will focus on that role.

David's statement about being a "regular dad" reminds us that being a dad doesn't have to be flashy or dramatic, but just loving, natural and, well, "regular." A real dad doesn't have all the answers. He does his best and still makes mistakes, but he loves his children so he keeps trying. He doesn't take himself too seriously, but he does take his role as dad seriously because he knows the positive influence he can have and, if he's not careful, the damage he could do. He wants to do a good job.

There are many books about raising children. This one is more about raising dads. This book will suggest ways to do that good job that nearly all fathers would like to do. As to the format of the book, there are five major elements to point out:

1. SELF-ESTEEM. Whether our children succeed in the long run, out in the big, broad world they will meet when they leave our care, depends a great deal on their self-esteem, their view of themselves. Yet there is no chapter in this book on self-esteem. Why not? Because as I outlined the book, I soon saw that the idea of enhancing our children's self-esteem was infused in the content matter of virtually every chapter.

NEARLY EVERYTHING WE DO WITH, TO, OR FOR OUR CHILDREN HAS AN EFFECT ON THE WAY THEY VIEW THEMSELVES.

Though there's no chapter on self-esteem, it may be that that's what this book is really about, after all. It will be mentioned over and over again as we discuss such things as discipline, love, communication, values, and decision making.

There is nothing more important a dad can instill in his children than a healthy view of themselves. Children with proper self-

confidence will make it through life. Without it, they will constantly flounder.

2. EXAMPLES. Since being a dad is a daily, down-to-earth,
practical task, I want this book, above all, to be practical and ap-
plicable. Stories and examples, mostly true incidents in my own or
other families, are used to illustrate principles under discussion. I
hope this will make the ideas clear enough that any dad reading the
book can see how to take the ideas off the pages and apply them
to the operation of their own homes.

3. KEY MOMENTS. In most of these examples, a point will be
made about the "key moment" involved. This is to help us identify
these significant moments of decision in our contact with our children, when the relationship will be either strengthened or weakened.

A KEY MOMENT IS A CRITICAL INSTANT WHEN WHAT IS DONE WILL IMPROVE AND ADVANCE THE RELATIONSHIP OR IT WILL HURT AND RETARD IT.

Life is filled with such opportunities. These moments come unex-
pectedly in the midst of our daily activities and recognizing them
is critical. If your child asks your help, you may face a key moment.
If you don't treat the issue as important, the child may feel that her
problems are not of concern to you. You will have failed at a key
moment and you may teach something you didn't want to teach—
that dad doesn't have time for his child.

If, on the other hand, you take the time (or set up a later time,
if you honestly don't have time now) and treat the matter as
worthy of your attention, you communicate to your child that she
is important to you. The relationship will be improved, the key moment handled correctly, and trust built.

Such opportunities occur often in my household of seven children;
on some days, they fly right and left. Sometimes they're obvious at
the moment, sometimes not clear until after the fact. At times I handle
them correctly; in other cases, not until later do I see what I should
have done.

The more we are aware of these key moments and how to use them correctly, the more we can improve our relationships with people we care for. Therefore, throughout this book, we'll talk a lot about key moments. I'll try to illustrate them sufficiently for you to recognize and react positively to them in your role as a dad. They can make a big difference.

4. DISCUSSION. Each chapter except the last one is followed with a section called TOPICS FOR DISCUSSION WITH YOUR WIFE. Here the concepts and ideas from that chapter are presented in open-ended question format for you to discuss with your spouse. (If you are a single parent, don't feel left out; just thinking through the questions will still be beneficial.) Such discussions will help clarify your views and help both of you to form practical plans for increased consistency and effectiveness in dealing with your children. You may find these discussions the greatest benefit of the book.

Since I'm just a "regular dad," I won't be able to give you many answers. But if I can cause you up to think about your role and discuss your views with your spouse, together you will come to conclusions and approaches that will benefit your family a great deal. After you've talked over these ideas with your wife, and perhaps jotted down a few goals for each chapter's topics, the ideal would be to talk with your children, if they are old enough, about your ideas. Explain your goals for your family, and get their input.

5. MAIN IDEAS. You've noticed in this preface another format element used in the book: capitalized main ideas sprinkled throughout the text. These are meant as a quick summary or review of major points being covered, and hopefully they increase readability.

FATHERHOOD IS A CONSTANT CHALLENGE AND AN EXCITING ONE.

Raising a family, in spite of being a heck of a lot of work, should be the most fun, rewarding thing a man does in his life. It is for me.

Love will go a long way toward establishing a positive relationship with your children. Love is where it all starts. But sometimes love isn't enough. Parents can love their children and still fail to communicate that love to them, fail to help them grow, and fail to be a positive force in their lives. Sometimes we just don't know how. In this book, we'll emphasize ways to put into action the good that a dad, even just a "regular dad," can do.

You might assume that, with seven children, I have been driven to being either an expert in these matters or a complete lunatic by now, but neither extreme is fully accurate. I doubt that I can really teach anyone much about being a good parent. But you can teach yourself, and if your wife will discuss these ideas with you, you will both be strengthened.

I hope this book will be a catalyst, and that the thinking it causes you to do will increase the value you place on your role as dad and help you to do a better job, no matter how well you already may be doing.

TABLE OF CONTENTS

15

A dad has to work at making the time, not just
  wait to "find it"

Teach children to question societal standards to the
   point where they can come to their
   own conclusions and lifestyle

1

Dad, Who Are You and What Good Are You Anyway?

Deep down, how do you feel about your role as dad? Do you have better things to do than to raise children? Do you think that it's really mother's work? Do you see the father's role in the family as significant or just peripheral?

Historically, our culture has relegated dads to a background role in child-rearing, but few would claim that as the ideal. Certainly some single, divorced, or widowed women raise wonderful children alone, as do some single men, but that doesn't mean it's the best situation. A parent needs all the help he or she can get, and a two-parent family is better, where both parents are committed to involved, responsible parenthood. Dad's role is as critical as mom's.

What is the role of fatherhood, beyond the biological function of procreation? Just what can a dad contribute to his children?

Perhaps we can gain insight into these questions by asking another: At what point does a man become a father?

There are a few obvious possibilities. Legally and biologically, a man becomes a father at conception. New life has been created, and in that moment a father is also formed.

Another view is that it's only at the birth of his child that a dad is really born, that only then does he begin to sense his responsibility for his new family.

There are some other "firsts" in a dad's life that contribute to his awareness of his role. It's said that no man is a true father until he bravely changes his first diaper. Or when he gets up in the middle of the night to comfort his crying baby, valiantly letting his wife sleep—which he will humbly remind her of several times the next. day.

Other events such as the child's first step, first word (especially if it's "da-da"), first day in school, his son's first shave, and his daughter's first date are also "creators" of fatherhood, because they force us to look at our children and our role in new ways. Our children don't stand still; they grow and advance. This causes us, as parents (just when we thought we were getting things figured out) to have to make adjustments. In this sense, we truly grow up with our children.

Beyond these events, I suggest four other major instances of growth and deepened insight into the fatherhood role.

THE FIRST GROWTH MOMENT OCCURS WHEN WE SUDDENLY BECOME AWARE OF HOW OUR CHILDREN VIEW US.

It's a heady feeling for a man to realize that he is now a force, and, yes, at times even a hero in a young person's life. It can also be quite sobering when we ponder the implications of how our children view us.

We may furrow our brows a little, wondering how well we measure up. We all want to be seen as having certain characteristics, and children are often wonderfully frank in telling us just how far we may be from living up to our inflated self-perceptions. One moment we're enjoying the fantasy of what great guys we are. The next, our balloon is harpooned by the sharp barb of innocent(?), youthful candor, such as when Angela, then three, said to me one day at the lunch table when I was having a little trouble with my soup, "Need a bib, daddy?"

Their candor can be funny, or sometimes not so funny. Either way, we learn a lot from our children as we discover how they perceive us.

SECOND, ONE OF THE BIGGEST STEPS

TOWARD GOOD FATHERHOOD COMES WITH THE REALIZATION THAT IT TAKES EFFORT TO DO THE JOB.

Fatherhood isn't a hobby that can be performed only when we feel like it or find time for it, like stamp collecting or ham radio. Being a dad, a good one, is a job that requires planning, dedication, and work.

Though fatherhood clearly has its rewards, it could be the toughest thing we've ever done. Attention, interest, energy, and time are all taken away from things we enjoy. Hopefully that doesn't make the task depressing or oppressive. But the role does have to be taken seriously. When a man notices that, and makes the necessary commitment, he's on his way to raising better children and enjoying them more besides.

THIRD, ANOTHER BIG STEP IS TAKEN WHEN WE REALIZE THAT MUCH OF THE ADVICE AIMED AT MOTHERS APPLIES IN ALMOST ALL CASES WITH EQUAL FORCE TO US AS FATHERS.

Our society casts mom in the role of the loving, nurturing, attentive parent, leaving "macho" dad only a supporting role. Much of the advice in magazines, newspapers, and parenting books seems directed more at mom than at dad. Some people, mostly men, seem to think this is just fine, that all is well if mom raises the kids while dad is merely the primary provider. But when a man realizes that there is much more to provide than income, that children are better off with two involved parents than one and a half, that a dad should be central, not auxiliary, to the rearing of his children, he takes another big step toward good fatherhood.

AND FOURTH, PERHAPS A MAN BECOMES A REAL DAD WHEN HE BECOMES

AWARE OF HIS OWN FATHER'S ROLE
IN HIS EARLY LIFE.

An eye-opening thought is the realization that the love you feel for your child must be similar to what your dad felt for you in your youth. From this moment on, you may never be the same because your perspective is changed, your vision expanded, your love for your own dad deepened. You may find yourself thinking about that relationship, wondering how your father felt about things, why he was the way he was, what his hopes and dreams were for you, his son.

You will surely find yourself in time doing many things the way your father did—perhaps things you swore you would never do. You might even find that you've developed a pot-belly and a bald spot like his, things that you were sure *you* were never going to get. It's a sobering experience.

A few years ago, I had an insight of unexpected emotion regarding this relationship with my own dad. It occurred when a small package arrived in the mail—a cassette tape recording.

First, a little background into my relationship with dad. Growing up on a small farm in Idaho, I was relatively close to my parents. We did quite a few things together as a family and I remember a lot of good times spent with my dad, hunting, fishing, and working together on the farm.

Just after my fourteenth birthday we sold the acreage and moved to the city. In my later teenage years, there was less to bind us together. I was finding my own way in life, as teenagers do, and parents didn't seem like a big part of my existence at the time. The teenage mind takes such relationships for granted, and I don't think I showed much real interest in my parents, although I never doubted that they cared a great deal for me and my sisters.

When I was eighteen, my folks started having problems. They finally separated and were later divorced. I blamed dad and I rejected him. College and other things soon took me out of state, so seeing him was rare. He remarried and, of course, I had no interest in his new family.

After my own marriage, my only contact with my dad was a twenty-minute annual visit when we were in town to visit mom, in an effort to keep him somewhat acquainted with his grandchildren. But these visits were strained, with little for me to talk with him about. Our lifestyles and interests were different and I still blamed him for the divorce.

However, in the last few years, with my "mellowing" forties approaching, I came to find it easier to talk to dad, and many of the old animosities seemed to lessen. Then my wife, as a surprise for me, asked him to record his life story—that's what was on the tape the mailman brought.

Listening to dad talk about his life on that tape was a moving experience for me. I had heard many of his stories before, as a boy, but enjoyed them again in the presence of my children, who had heard none of them. But most startling to me was dad's admission on the tape that he had made a lot of mistakes in life, the main one being losing my mom. This touched me deeply. I had never heard dad express any remorse over the divorce and I assumed he had none. Suddenly I saw my dad in a new light. The twenty-two-year old wound has been healed.

My point in mentioning this experience is that my role as a parent has been enhanced since I can now better relate to my own dad and see him as a human being—a regular dad growing and changing and struggling with his own problems and feelings.

While you may not have or have need for such a dramatic turnabout in your relationship with your own father, it's likely that, at some point, you will gain appreciation for his role in your life. This increase of love for your dad can only benefit your relationship with your own children.

Listening to that tape was a key moment in my life, a point where a relationship changed. On that occasion, I believe I handled my key moment correctly, because the emotion I felt and the letter I wrote my dad did restore and improve the relationship immensely.

IN SPITE OF ALL ELSE YOU MAY DO, YOUR ROLE AS FATHER IS THE MOST IMPORTANT IN YOUR LIFE.

There is nothing you are likely to do that will have as lasting an influence as will your work as a father. Other roles in life have much less significance by comparison. If I succeed as a dad, all my other roles are enhanced. If I fail, all the others are lessened.

Though the act of siring a child identifies a man as a dad, interest, thought, and introspection are necessary to cause him to do a good job at fathering. Oh, it's true that there are "natural" dads, guys who have never read a single book on parenting but who have a marvelous relationship with their children. For others—perhaps most of us, it isn't so natural—we have to "think our way to better fatherhood." Our desires are right; we just need some ideas and motivation along the way.

Getting those ideas and that motivation takes effort. Not that it requires a Ph.D. in child psychology. After all, a "regular dad" is the goal. But we can all benefit from new ideas on how to be better at our job. Observation of other dads, reflecting on our own father's role in our life, and reading some of the many parenting books are ways to get ideas. But mainly our desires and interest make the difference. We have to not only be interested in our children and want the best for them, but be willing to share our life and our time with them.

Topics For Discussion With Your Wife

(Keep in mind that there are no "right" answers for any of these discussion items that follow each chapter. Both parties should agree in advance to be honest, but that the discussion should be kept positive and for the purpose of improvement. Both must try hard to listen and understand the other. If you are a single parent, you can still benefit from carefully considering the questions.)

1. How clear are we at defining our roles with our children? Do we both feel good about distinctions that exist between the role of the father and that of the mother? How much overlap in roles is there? Are there areas where one or both of us feels uncomfortable or feels that some redefinition of roles ought to occur?

2. How supportive are we of one another in our roles? Does each of us feel the support of the other? How could such support be made more clear?

3. How do we honestly feel about how close we are coming to fulfilling our roles well?

4. What are some of the good effects each of us has on the children? Are there negative effects that one party has observed and that the other doesn't see?

5. How do we feel about input and critique from each other in the roles we play? Are we willing to learn from the other's viewpoint? When critique is given, are there preferred methods, times, and places to give it? Do we have clear ground rules for such discussions?

6. How much in agreement are we on the ideas in this chapter? Are we working together? Have we identified areas of difference and are we able to talk about them? Are there major areas we need to discuss further in the future?

2

A "Last Letter"

Dear Angela, David, Taylor, Matthew, Geneal, Alysa, and Aaron,

Some institutions I'm aware of sponsor a series of lectures called the "Last Lectures." Speakers in this series are asked to deliver the speech they would give if they knew it was to be their last chance to leave a message with the world. Calling it his "last lecture" gets a speaker to think hard about the most important ideas he wants to leave his audience.

I'm using this idea in writing to the seven of you. I've asked myself: If I were to be able to leave, in writing, just one letter to my children, what would my message be? What would be the most important thoughts I would share?

Asking oneself such a question is sobering. It's a little bit like asking, "If you knew you would die tomorrow, what would you do today?"

In a sense, it's an impossible question to answer realistically. There are so many worthwhile ways to spend time that it's hard to single out any specific way as the most important. As soon as we say, "Oh, I'd go skiing," or "I'd climb a mountain and just sit and think," we realize we would be leaving out a lot of other good things such as spending time with people we love. Any choice we make precludes lots of others.

Therefore, many people answer something like, "I would do what I regularly do—go to work or school—but probably spend a little more time with my family." This answer indicates an acceptance on the part of these people that their daily lives are perfectly adequate. They find meaning in their regular routine; nothing spectacular is needed to make them feel fulfilled.

I feel much the same way about this letter to you. Virtually everything I would say to you children I have already said in different ways on different occasions or have tried to show you through our daily lives together. Writing my thoughts down as if it's the last message I would leave you makes things more clear and more final, but it doesn't really change the nature of the message into anything new or spectacular.

A dad has hopes and dreams, just like anyone else does. But I wasn't always a dad. As a youth, I had what are probably the standard visions of becoming famous and rich, being a world traveler, making key decisions, and doing important things for mankind. When we get a little older, start a family, and enter the work place, our lives get very busy, and most of us find that a few of our youthful dreams get covered over in the dust of daily bustle. Others of the dreams of youth seem less important and are replaced by new ideals and goals because our values change. And many of those new values, dreams, and goals involve you, my children.

The dreams of my youth were often selfish; they centered on how much money I could spend, the places I could travel to, how much glory I could get for the heroic acts I might perform. Now, more of my hopes are for what *you* will do. Not that I've lost all of my personal dreams—which I hope I never do—or gotten over all of my selfishness—which I hope I will do. But I now see things from a different perspective.

What are my dreams for you? Basically, that you will remain good people. Whether or not you become "great" people, in terms of worldly fame, fortune, or influence doesn't matter to me. But I want you to be great in the things that mean the most.

Someday every one of you will be all grown up and leave our home to live your own lives. When that happens and those final apronstrings are cut (that's the standard image of cutting loose from moms, but what's the image for dads?) nearly all you will have to take with you will be memories.

And of what will those memories be? Well, here are some feelings and impressions I hope you will retain from your years in this home, a few positive memories your dad wanted most to give you:

First is love. Parents *have* to love their kids, don't they? It's just human nature, expected and required of them, and most parents do love their children. But that doesn't mean there won't be times when those same children won't feel loved.

I hope you will go away from home feeling that you were really loved in spite of the times when your dad was upset, tired, angry, or unfair. Especially I hope you still felt loved when *you* were the ones upset, tired, angry, or unfair—at those times when you were the least lovable. When you needed it most, I want you to have felt supported and deeply loved.

Particularly, I trust that you will know that you were loved just for being you, not because of your achievements, accomplishments, good deeds, good grades, or good looks, but just because of your unique "you-ness." In our house, you never needed to earn the love of your parents. That love was always there and it will always be there in the future. Nothing you could do would change that. You will always be part of us.

Six of you were old enough to notice how much love Aaron, our seventh, brought into our home at his birth. Though you aren't able to remember your *own* receptions into our household, the truth is that each one of you were received the same way. From the oldest to the youngest, each of you brought great joy into our home. So first, I want you to remember love.

Next, when you someday pack up your treasures, your junk, your memories, and your life, and carry them out our door for good, I want you to have good memories of growing up within these walls. I want you to remember family activities and traditions, and feel that you were a part of them. I hope you will remember the many good hours we squeezed out of our busy lives to spend together working, playing, talking, laughing, crying, loving, and, yes, even arguing, for in that way did we sometimes get to know one another the best of all. And I want you to feel that none of those events and activities would have been the same if each of you had not been part of our family.

Another memory I wish for you is that you will be able to look back at the times of dad's and mom's chastisements and concede that these were mostly done for your own good, as well as we could perceive it at the time. Not that we were perfect or always unselfish—we're human too—but we cared for you and your growth and safety. Maybe we were sometimes too distrustful, too harsh, or, worst of all, too old-fashioned. But if you can know that our overreactions occurred because we cared, it may help.

Knowing full well that our human weakness sometimes allowed us to use unrighteous dominion over you, I hope you realize that the greater part of our discipline was done out of love. If you don't recognize or believe this, we might have unknowingly taught you to be a bully just because you're bigger than someone else, to use your authority against those younger and smaller than you, just to get your way.

Perhaps you will also remember your dad's saying "I'm sorry," when I knew I had been wrong. Maybe you can forgive me for those other times when I was sure I was right, and it turned out I was wrong even then.

When that day comes that you are on your own, I want you to take with you the strongest possible self-esteem. I'm hopeful that you will mostly remember your successes, and that you will think of your dad as someone who tried to help you recognize your self-worth by giving you tasks at which you could succeed, even if you sometimes needed a little pushing. I hope you felt our urging to grow and develop, so that when you eventually achieved full independence, you were ready for the responsibility. I hope you didn't feel we tried to unduly hold you back and keep you our "babies" for our own needs.

I hope you will not much remember your failures because that may mean that either we or you made too much of them. In those inevitable disappointments, the lessons I expected you to learn are as trite as they are true:

Failure is as normal as flies in summer.

Failing at a task isn't the same as failing as a person.

As long as you get up and try again, you are not a failure.

You, each of you, can take on the world and achieve whatever you want to. Your mother and I wanted you to know that, which is why we constantly found ways to push you gently but firmly into that sometimes scary world. When we didn't let you offer some flimsy excuse for poor behavior, we wanted you to know that you can't hide behind anything—not even your parents' faults or other deficiencies in your upbringing as excuses for not being successful in the things that matter.

In our home, I hope you had opportunities to come to know your own unique gifts and strengths, some of which, at the time, even your parents couldn't see, and that you were allowed the space to grow in your own way rather than being forced into some mold to fulfill your parents' preconceived notions or to protect their image, ego, or social needs.

I hope your self-esteem developed sufficiently in our home for you to have learned tolerance for the views and lifestyles of others, so that you are prepared to bring help, not hostility, to a troubled world—aid, not acrimony.

Another of my hopes is that you will look back on our home and remember it as a place where you could come to get respite from the storms of life, where you could bring your problems, hopes and dreams, friends and lost puppies. I meant it to be the one place where you always felt welcomed, not nagged or badgered, judged or threatened, a place to hide out for awhile on bad days so you could gather strength to go back into the storm.

I hope, too, that you will remember experiences in our home that helped you learn to look at the world in a realistic, yet optimistic way, understanding that nothing is perfect but that life is good and must not be run away from.

Our dinner-table and late-nights discussions about all manner of things—science, religion, history, current events, teachers, and neighbors—should have helped you gain confidence about the world and your place in it, and be ready to face it. I trust that, when you leave our care, you will have learned to support yourself in a satisfactory way without becoming a crass materialist who sees money as the most important thing in life.

I hope you will have learned how to handle, not hide, from the inevitable conflicts that arise in life, even with—perhaps especially with—those you love most. Learning how to communicate your own deep feelings and how to listen to and accept the feelings of others is a lifelong task.

In short, I'm hopeful that you will think of your years at home as years of practicing how to live. Perhaps the selective filter of your mind will mercifully elevate to the top of your memory the time your dad spent on the important things in life, like digging a grave for the cat who got under the wheels of the car, sanding pinewood racers for Cub Scout derbies, and leaving secret notes in your school desks when your mom and I went to parent-teacher conferences, and will push to a lower level the petty carping—and I did my share—about the small stuff like messy rooms, imperfect math papers, not getting to bed on time, and wearing mismatched clothes to church.

The greatest compliment each of you could pay your dad is to take charge of your life and live it in a significant way. The greatest compliment your dad can pay you is to admit that most of the concepts I've listed here that I hope you've learned in our home, I actually learned myself because of, and along with you.

Love,
Dad

Topics For Discussion With Your Wife

1. What do we think of the idea of writing "last letters" to our children? (Not that a letter such as this one need actually be delivered to your children, especially if they are too young to read it, but writing one is a great way of clarifying what you want for your children.) If we were to write such a letter, what would it say?

2. If we were each to write such a letter, we would probably emphasize different things. Are these ideas and goals *all* compatible? Can they all be worked in? Are there areas which we feel can be handled by one parent better than the other and that ought to be left to that one primarily? Are there some that must be jointly handled?

3. How much in agreement are we on the ideas in this chapter? Are we working together? Have we identified areas of difference, and are we able to talk about them? Are there major areas we need to discuss further at a future time

3

Love Comes First

In our culture, we have many things about love all mixed up. Love connotes softness, tenderness, and warmth, and somehow, over the last several hundred years of Western civilization, these traits have come to be thought of mainly as feminine characteristics. Since men carry the cultural stereotype of hard, stern, and tough creatures, males must not be capable of love.

Nonsense. Almost any man who has seen his newborn feels love. A dad who, coming in the door, finds his two-year old running to him saying, "Daddy, daddy, you're home!" knows what love is.

BEING LOVING HAS NOTHING TO DO WITH FEMININITY OR MASCULINITY. IT HAS TO DO WITH HUMANITY.

Those who don't feel love are less than fully human. Now, whether we dads always know how to show it might be another matter, but feel love we do.

But our culture has assigned us dads the "tough," disciplinarian kinds of roles. "Just wait till your father gets home," moms have said to their children for centuries. Our acceptance of this traditional role of judge and executioner has perhaps caused us to think that we had to be the tough guy in the family, showing no emotion or love.

This unfair assignment and the cultural impetus behind it may have contributed to the difficulty that some dads have in showing affection and love. Perhaps men have concluded that showing love is a weakness, only done through romantic Valentine's cards, drippy sentiment, or excessive tenderness which is unbecoming the male.

Furthermore, our culture expects males, above all else they do, to succeed in the hard, cold, "real" world. We're applauded for success in making money, wielding power, and in being decisive. We're expected to "take charge," to always be rational and strong. It's not hard to conclude that nurturing is only for women and that men ought to be interested in things other than families and children.

So you see what we have to overcome, dads, if we want to fully develop our capabilities to love, and especially our abilities to *show* love.

Besides these cultural hindrances to our showing our loving and nurturing sides, there's one other big roadblock in our own thinking. Many of us have learned to view love as something to be earned, and we unwittingly inflict this philosophy on our families. In the work place we learn that effort is rewarded with money, prestige, power, or promotion. And we come to think that all rewards need to be earned. Soon this idea may carry over to our ways of showing love to our children. But love isn't a reward, it's a right.

Love that's a reward is conditional. People receive conditional love when they earn it, and they're all too aware that it can be lost when their performance drops off. Our approval, therefore, becomes one that is not of *people* so much as it is of their *achievements*.

Much of the world does work on the earned reward system, and it's not a bad system, in its place. When an employee fails to do his tasks properly, his reward, in the form of pay, can be taken away. When an entertainer fails to please enough people, the low ticket sales at his concerts will force him out of the market; his reward will automatically disappear. But when we apply this "earn-it-and-you'll-get-it" idea to love, the system becomes a bad one.

LOVE ISN'T SOMETHING THAT HAS TO BE EARNED BY OUR CHILDREN.

We don't take love away from people because they don't do all the things we would like them to. Such conditional love just isn't worth much; it isn't to be trusted because of the ease with which it can be taken away. Therefore, it means little to the recipient.

In the New Testament (Luke 15:11-24) we read of a man who knew how to give another kind of love, one that was not conditioned on anything. It's the story told by Jesus of the prodigal son. A man with two sons divided his wealth between them. The elder son stayed at home and continued the kind of life he always had, that of serving his father and working with him. The younger son, however, became prodigal, or extravagant, with his new-found wealth. He left the area, went to a land where he was unknown and could "live it up," and spent his inheritance in a reckless and immoral manner.

Quickly impoverished, he was reduced to working as a laborer, experiencing hunger to the point of even wanting to eat the husks of the grain he fed the swine of the man he worked for. Realizing that he had made a great mistake, the son decided to return home to ask his father if he could become one of his servants.

At this point in the story we learn a great deal about the father. In verse 20 we're told: "But when he was a great way off, his father saw him, and had compassion, and ran, and fell on his neck, and kissed him."

Here is a dad who knew how to give love. In no way did the son deserve or merit this kind of acceptance. He had earned absolutely nothing unless, perhaps, condemnation. But the father gave love just because he felt it toward his son. This was no achievement-based, conditional love. The story stands as one of the greatest parables in the scriptures designed to show us how to love.

How does that father's love compare with what we regular dads sometimes give our regular kids? How do we deal with them when their halos slip a little and they don't obey as fast as we would like? What about when they're smart-mouthed, lazy, demanding, ungrateful? Do we withhold our approval—which our children may well interpret as withholding our love—until they merit the approval? Do we make them earn our love?

What do we convey to our children when we get down on them too much for poor grades, poor sports skills, staying up late, or clothing styles? Are we sure they don't perceive us as not loving them?

"But," you say, "that isn't what I intend. I'm just trying to show them that they can do better." Well, whether or not lack of love is what you intend, it may be exactly what's conveyed.

THE MESSAGE RECEIVED IS WHAT'S IMPORTANT, NOT THE MESSAGE SENT.

When Joey was nine, he signed up for city league softball for the summer. At the first game, because dad was watching from the sidelines, Joey tried his best to play well. It ought to be pretty obvious what dad's key moments were, especially if Joey did not show potential for a future in the major leagues. You can imagine how Joey felt when he heard his dad shout, "Way to go, Joey. Good try," compared to what he felt when he heard, "Oh, come on, Joey. Don't be a klutz!"

If a child feels he isn't quite measuring up, he can very easily feel rejected and unloved. I've seen signs of these feelings in my own children when I've been critical. And though, in *my* mind, my criticism had nothing to do with my love for them, in *their* minds, at that moment, it seems to have.

There is another form of conditional love that is more subtle but just as harmful. This form has nothing to do with threats of rejections but with compliments. When we compliment our children because of *what they do*, not *what they are*, isn't our love conditional?

Think about it. When do we compliment our children? Usually when they've done something good, right? So our most innocent praise can be misconstrued. "Gee, Richard, that's great that you got an A in math," or "I sure love you, Janice, when you help me like that," may be meant as aids to increasing the math or helping behaviors, but such praise may convey to the children that they're only loved when they do the things we like.

Don't get me wrong; such compliments are better than no compliments. But how much better if we would just walk up to Richard or Janice one day and say, "I really love you, and I'm glad you're in our family."

If we can do that when they haven't done a blessed thing to earn the comment, then we've told them in a subtle way that, no matter what the behavior, they are loved.

I believe that such unconditional love is necessary for the development of proper self-esteem in children. If we base our love for them on their achievements, *or if they think we do*, they will never think themselves quite worthy.

ACHIEVEMENT-BASED LOVE IS DANGEROUS BECAUSE IT CAN BE LOST IF PERFORMANCE DROPS.

Children who feel they're loved only for what they do will always fear that failing will lose that love. This view will also affect their love for us because it creates distrust in them. They're not sure whether they can fully accept and reciprocate our love if they fear we might change the rules on them. Maybe they're succeeding now but what if they don't put on a good showing later?

On the whole, children are a rather insecure lot, though the degree varies with the child and with the situation. They will tend to feel insecure about our acceptance, even when, from our point of view, they have no need to, if we don't take care to show that our love isn't conditional. We must make an extra effort to let our children know that we love them without question, without condition, and whether or not they are good at doing the things we like done.

In our efforts to teach our children responsibility and to get them to do what we ask them to do, we're allowed to use various honest means to get them to conform to our wishes. It must be clear, however, that there is one lever we will never use: we will never withdraw our love.

This one fact must be made absolutely clear to children. They must know that they will never be disowned or removed from the fellowship of the family, no matter what.

One way of insuring that our children know that they are an inseparable part of us is to make sure they know they are very, very special to us. A short story by Erma Bombeck tells of three young men of high school and college age attending their mother's funeral. During the services, Chuck, the oldest son, takes out a letter from his mom and secretly rereads the part where she tells him, "Since this letter is for no one's eyes but yours, I can tell you that I always loved you best."

Beside him, Steve, the middle son, remembers his letter, which said, "You must have suspected, but I will say it anyway. I have always loved you best." And Tim, the fourteen-year-old at the end of the row, ponders the letter his mother left him, beginning, "A mother is not supposed to have favorites, but I have always loved you best."

None of these young men knows, of course, about the other letters, and each one of them goes his way feeling better because of this special secret he shared with his mother, that he was her favorite. The point is clear that each boy has benefited greatly from his view that he was so special to her. (Erma Bombeck, "I Loved You Best," *Reader's Digest*, January 1984)

Obviously, this mother stretched the meaning of the word "favorite" to have each son feel a special relationship. In the strictest sense, the word can't stretch quite that far. But this is a home we're running, not a court room.

This concept may not appeal to you. It certainly didn't to me the first time I read of it, years ago, in a book on child rearing. This writer made a very provocative point:

A PARENT SHOULD MAKE EACH CHILD THINK HE OR SHE IS NUMBER ONE.

No matter what has to be done to convey that idea to the child, this author indicated it must be done. Only if they compare notes and come to you for an explanation—which is very unlikely—do you tell them that Jill is your favorite because she is the oldest; Sally is your favorite because she has the curliest hair; John is your favorite because he is the smallest. (Notice that none of these statements is based on anyone's achievements but just on unique natural qualities.) (*Child Sense* by William E. Homan, M.D., New York: Bantam Books, Inc., 1970)

At the time, I found this idea disturbing. It seemed deceitful and competitive and went against my concepts of parental fairness. But the more I thought about it, the more I came to see value in the concept of letting each child feel special to the parent and not just special in an item or two, but special above the other children, the number one child.

One of the reasons I came to see value in the idea is that a few years ago, I took an informal poll on this subject. I asked several young adults whether, when they were growing up, they felt that their parents had favorites, and, if so, who that favorite was. The answers were most revealing.

Almost all of those questioned at first answered that their parents were fair. But this turned out to be their adult response as to what their parents *intended*. When pressed just a little more, most of them said they hadn't felt that way at the time.

Very seldom did I find people who felt their parents were, in their recollections, perfectly fair to all, although they almost universally said they thought their parents tried to be. Almost all of them gave answers in one of the following categories:

1. Yes, my parents had a favorite, and I was it.

or

2. Yes, my parents had a favorite, and it was Sam (or Sue).

Since this was just an informal survey in the course of several conversations, I wasn't able to ask the parents of these people how *they* had felt, but I would bet that almost all of those parents thought they were being fair to all their children, and that there were no favorites. Yet the young adults I talked to often admitted that they came away feeling that there was a favorite, and all of them except those in category one above felt a little bitter about it.

THE POINT IS THAT
FAIRNESS DOESN'T WORK.

Now, what shall we do with this information in becoming better dads? Rather than spend time arguing that we are meticulously fair to all, I think we would be better off recognizing that most children are vulnerable enough to frequently feel slighted, whether or not the "fair" facts warrant it, and that they will conclude that they are not special to their parents unless those parents do something to show them otherwise.

If you can find ways to tell or show each child that he is number one with you, the insecurity every child feels at some points in his young life might be somewhat counteracted. It's very often their own insecurity that causes the problem. Nonetheless, it's a real problem in the mind of the child, one not to be overcome by our preaching how fair we are. At thirty-five, your child may understand that you were fair, but at five or fifteen, when he needs your support the most, he just may feel you like a sibling better.

If you can make it clear that you love your child just because he's yours, not because of what he does or accomplishes, and at the same time that he—each one—is your "favorite," you will have managed two very important things.

Remember: Jenny is your favorite just because she's your first daughter—not because she's the hardest worker and the smartest in school—that would be loving her for her actions instead of for herself. And Tommy is also your favorite because he has the cheeriest laugh and the deepest dimples.

Since, as was pointed out early in this chapter, our culture seems to place love in the category of feminine things, we ought to look at how love can be shown by a regular dad. Here are some possibilities:

1. LIKE YOUR CHILDREN. Let's assume that you love your children. But do you like them? Is there affection in your home? Affection is a broad term, but I'm going to narrow it somewhat to mean more than just loving, but liking our children.

I THINK A LOT OF CHILDREN FEEL LOVED, BUT THEY DON'T FEEL LIKED.

They don't feel affection and acceptance. They don't feel fully welcome in your presence or that you like them to be around you. They're sure you see them as a bother, and they don't feel like an equal to you.

What about it, dad? Do you like your children? If the answer to that is yes, then be sure they know it.

But if the honest answer is no, then maybe it's because you don't really know them. And getting to know them requires work and time. Are you willing to supply those?

2. TELL THEM SO. If we like people, or love them, or both, we ought to say so now and then. You've probably heard the story of the old man leaving his wife's funeral, and saying, "Ah, I loved that

gal. And in fifty years of marriage, once or twice I came close to telling her so." We've all heard less amusing stories about people who grew up never hearing their parents express love to their children. Usually, it seems, it's the dads who never get around to saying "I love you." Some dads claim that's because they never heard love expressed when they were growing up, and they just don't know how to say it.

NO MATTER WHAT YOUR UPBRINGING WAS, WHETHER YOUR DAD EVER TOLD YOU HE CARED, WHETHER ANYBODY SHOWED YOU ANY LOVE OR NOT, YOU CAN STILL TELL YOUR OWN CHILDREN YOU LOVE THEM.

Just be a man, open your mouth, and do it. Today!

If you find such words too hard to say, write them down. A note to a child is often much more meaningful than a passing word anyway. It doesn't have to be a long letter like that in chapter 2. Just a quick note that says, "Suzie, you're my favorite first grader; Love, Dad," will bring a response that's well worth your trouble. You'll probably get a beautiful picture using all the colors in the crayon box in return.

A note to a fifteen-year old might not get you any acknowledgement at all, but there will be an inner response felt by that child nevertheless.

The first time Zina wrote love notes to each child at Christmas time and put them in their stockings, we were amazed to see the children sit down and read the notes on Christmas morning before looking at anything under the tree.

I believe in writing or saying how you feel, but it's certainly not the only worthwhile means of communication. There are other ways to "say it," too.

"Arnold, I sure enjoyed going to the ball game with you," is a way of saying "I like being around you," and that equates with love.

A novel way of indirectly telling how a dad feels about his children is to say, as I've sometimes said at the dinner table: "Everybody just stop and think for a minute how strange our family would be if Matthew weren't in it, and never had been. Wouldn't our family be different?"

Sincere praise is also a great way to tell people you like them. A typical dad, though, probably praises less than he condemns. I don't know why it's easier to notice—and mention—the plate that passed through a son's dishpan hands and still had a bit of food on it than all the others that were clean, but it seems to be the case, unless we work on the problem.

The many right things our children do may go unnoticed while the few foul-ups get our attention and comments. Keeping track of comments for a day or two is a way to see if I'm right that we do less praising than criticizing. I dare you to make that study. It might change your tune to one of praise, and you'll have to criticize less. And remember to praise sometimes just for being.

3. SHOW THEM. As necessary as it is to tell our children of our love *and* our liking for them, sometimes words are cheap.

IF WE WANT TO SHOW LOVE TO OUR CHILDREN, WE'LL HAVE TO SPEND TIME WITH THEM.

Watching, listening, asking about their interests, and letting our children take up our time, especially when we'd really like to read the paper, are ways to truly show interest in them.

During the winter when our Angela was nine, she asked to go ice skating. We agreed to wait until after Christmas when we were less busy. The mistake I made was to expand—in my own mind—this activity to include all of the children. Winter sniffles set in right after the holidays, and there wasn't a Saturday when someone wasn't down with a cold. At last, by late February, we found a bright, sunny Saturday when everybody was well, and we headed for the outdoor rink. Alas, we found that the ice had softened. The rink was closed for the season.

In her disappointment, Angela lost no time in telling me that I had made a big mistake in including all the family in the plans. Not that she minded others coming along, but their sicknesses had prevented her from going skating at all. Though my mistake was innocent,

I learned a lesson about planning and setting aside time for important things. (A trip to the roller-skating rink came as close as possible to saving the day.)

Showing our children we love them requires thinking ahead and organizing our time, so that we can show them we care.

4. TOUCH THEM. We usually don't touch people we don't like. Love includes touching. Not that non-touchers can't love, of course, but touching certainly helps express love and make it felt.

But touching is another of those cultural problems. Most American men don't feel comfortable with the southern European double cheek-kissing kind of greeting. Anything beyond a handshake between males is unnatural to most American men, even between family members. Yet we watch macho athletes patting and hugging each other on national TV and we think that looks natural enough. There must be something about the context.

AN EMBRACE BETWEEN 250-POUND FOOTBALL PLAYERS IS OK, BUT A DAD'S QUICK HUG OF A TEENAGE SON IS SUSPECT. MAYBE YOU CAN FIGURE IT OUT; I CAN'T.

Outside of these TV oddities, we seem to feel that men don't touch. We have a vague fear of perverted sexual feelings so we don't touch our boys. Certainly a teenage boy who hasn't been touched by his dad is going to find it startling at first. Let's hope you can start touching much sooner. Some dads still kiss their boys goodnight though these boys are in their teens. It's natural to all concerned because they got an early start and just never quit.

But even if you didn't get that early start, it isn't too late. Just don't shock your boy by starting with the hug. Try something less formal, like the hand slaps so in vogue today, slaps on the back, and other playful touching. Wrestling is good too, if you can still pin your opponent. Work your way up to walking down the hall once in a while with your hand on your son's shoulder and having it feel natural to both of you. Your goal could be at least one real hug before he graduates from high school!

If you weren't raised in such a way—and most of us weren't, I'm sure—touching will seem odd at first but it can be done. Touching is natural. *Not* touching is what's unnatural. While I don't suppose it's necessary to go to the full embrace every time your kid comes home after school, there is a time for appropriate touching of your children, be they boys or girls.

I read of one family where back rubs are given to one another regularly. This is their accepted way of showing concern for one another. You may not want to make a ritual out of this, but I noticed that, once we started giving one another mini-back rubs, our children soon asked for them, and now often massage one another. Besides feeling good these rubdowns are a valid way of saying, "I like you."

5. SUPPORT THEM. One of the ways that children discover that we really don't quite value them as equals is when we don't support them in the things they do.

WE NEED TO SUPPORT CHILDREN
IN THEIR INTERESTS AND DECISIONS,
ESPECIALLY AFTER THE FACT.

This means that we might counsel with them before a decision, but when it's made, even when it went against our hopes, our responsibility is to help our children make the most of whatever results may come.

If Sam saves his money for a baseball mitt when his dad think he ought to use his brother's hand-me-down, a little counsel to get him to think it through is sufficient. If, after that, the boy still wants a stiff, new, "better" one that he can break in himself, then dad ought to step back and let him save the money. How else can he learn to make decisions?

Another way to show love through after-the-fact support is by ignoring mistakes, especially public ones, made by our children. Suppose you have taken your little boy to buy a hamburger and he's spilled his drink. The lecture you will be tempted to give won't teach him a thing. Treating it lightly and ordering another drink for him will. It's the same thing you would do for another adult; your boy knows it, and he feels your support in an embarrassing moment.

6. PUSH THEM. Sometimes we think—and our children think—we don't love them because we don't help them enough. We don't do everything for them.

Statements like, "But Lori's dad drives her to school *every* day," will probably induce a little guilt in you, though it has nothing directly to do with whether either you or Lori's dad are "good" dads. But it is a key moment, in which you have to pause and decide if you are honestly neglecting your child or if this is just a chance to strengthen in her the idea that she is perfectly capable of getting to school by walking and that you're proud of her for not being a crybaby about it.

IT ISN'T NECESSARILY LOVING TO DO EVERYTHING FOR YOUR CHILDREN THAT THE COMBINED NEIGHBORHOOD PARENTS DO. AND IT ISN'T ALWAYS GOOD FOR THE CHILDREN.

Certainly we need to help them, but not necessarily by performing all the standard parental goodies for them.

If we fall into that guilt trap because of Lori's dad, we have succumbed to the erroneous view I mentioned at the start of this chapter—that love is soft. Love can be hard, meaning we need to let our children learn to do for themselves, even when we'd like to help them. At various points, we even need to push them into learning by doing, for their own good.

Topics For Discussion With Your Wife

1. How am I, as a dad, at expressing my love? Is it clear that, however it's done, my children know I do love them? How could I make that more clear?
2. How clear are we in our own minds about unconditional love for our children? How certain are we that we would never withdraw our love?
3. How clear is it to each child that our love is unconditional? Are

there insecurities in certain of our children that tell us we ought to give particular emphasis to showing more love to this one or that one?

4. How are we at praising and complimenting? How are compliments given, just because our children exist, rather than for what they do?

5. What do we think of the idea of letting each child feel like he, or she, is number one with us? How far are we willing to go to let each child feel special? How did each of us feel about our positions in the family when we were growing up? What effect did this have on us?

6. How does each of us show our children that we love them? What more could we do? How much supporting and pushing do we do? How do we feel about touching?

7. How much in agreement are we on the ideas in this chapter? Are we working together? Have we identified areas of difference, and are we able to talk about them? Are there major areas we need to discuss further at a future time?

4

Traditions and Memories

The lower canyon of the Provo River is but a five-minute drive from our home. This stretch of the river is regularly stocked with eight-to-ten inch rainbow trout, and several evenings each summer find me and my children there for a few minutes of fishing. On most nights we pull in one or two of those rainbows. At dusk one September evening several years ago we were nearly ready to leave for home, having had no bites all night. I cast out one more time and gave the pole to Taylor, who was then four or five years old, to hold, while Angela and David and I stood behind him. Suddenly something bigger than the normal pan-sized fish took the bait. We raised to the top of the water a trout that looked to be twenty inches long!

In my haste to help my son land him—having no net, I had to try to get my hands around him as we brought him to shore—we pulled the line too hard and the small swivel holding the hook, not made for such loads, bent open. The fish was gone, and I was devastated.

My children looked at me in wonder as I expressed my agitation at losing the fish. At first I was just a frustrated fisherman, angry at myself at not being more skillful. (Fortunately, in that key moment, I had the sense not to blame Taylor.)

In the next few minutes, my emotion turned to melancholy. I felt that catching that fish would have been a highlight in my children's lives and a bond between them and me, and the chance had been lost. I was disheartened.

It was now nearly dark and we started for the car. But, on the way, thinking that the evening might be somewhat salvaged if we could catch a regular-sized fish, I put on another hook and cast in once more about fifty feet downstream, under a small bridge.

How surprised I was to immediately feel another big strike! This time I was considerably more careful and we landed a beautiful nineteen-inch rainbow trout. Surely it must have been the same one. We were all ecstatic. I didn't realize how much my earlier concern had affected the children until one of them said, "Now you feel better, huh, dad?"

The evening was a success and the memory of the big fish under the bridge is still in our family, made even more memorable perhaps because we had almost failed.

A FAMILY IS MORE THAN A COLLECTION OF PEOPLE WHO LIVE IN THE SAME BUILDING.

A family is a group of people working, loving, learning, growing and maybe even fishing together—people who, over the years, come to have a collection of shared memories and traditions that help bind them and make them feel part of the family unit. There are probably few things that give a child a greater sense of identity than being part of a memory. It gives him a structure to build his own life on.

Some of these traditions and memories are accidental. No one plans to have the car get wrecked, the cat die, or a gallon of milk slip from dad's hands on the way to the refrigerator, to name but three "unforgettables" that have happened in our family. Yet, each of these and many others provide a binder that our children sometimes refer to with varying degrees of nostalgia. The spilling of the milk gets referred to the most, since, on that day, dad had the grace, before mopping it up, to dance around in the mess he had made, providing a good show for everyone at the lunch table.

Besides the accidentals, there are memories and traditions that ought to be cultivated and planned as part of the heritage you will provide your family. Just as cultures, nations, regions, and cities have traditions, so can families have traditions of significance.

CHILDREN NEED TO GROW UP FEELING
THAT THEY'RE PART OF A FAMILY
THAT'S SPECIAL IN SOME WAYS.

Not in too many ways, mind you—children don't like to feel *too* different from their friends—but a family should be unique and special in a few important areas. At slumber parties I've heard my young children warning their friends about my silly bedtime stories in a way that tells me that they enjoy them and want to share them with their friends. The uniqueness probably doesn't lie with the stories themselves since they're essentially quite boring, except for the bit of tickling at the end.

Such simple things as Bre'r Rabbit stories at bedtime illustrate that traditions don't have to be elaborate. Simplicity is just as memorable as extravagance as long as the experience is a worthy one. Think of your own childhood. You will likely remember as many small, seemingly insignificant events, traditions, and experiences, as bigger ones. These small matters give savor to your memory and help you feel a part of something. They're part of your heritage, and helped shape who you are today.

When I think back on those early years in my own life, I recall the hunting and fishing, the camping trips, farm work, trips to town, the Fourth of July fireworks show my parents put on for neighbors and friends, the firecrackers my cousin and I ordered every summer from a magazine, my 4-H pigs and chickens, teasing my two sisters, praying for a horse (and getting the answer to my prayer in my dad's pasturing his cousin's horse for a summer during which I saddled and rode him exactly once), conversations with friends, impressions of neighbors, visits with grandparents, and attendance at funerals, to name a few. Some of these were "big" events, planned and programmed; others were spontaneous and insignificant at the time.

Just as you have numerous memories from your youth, your children will look back and remember being a part of your family. While much of what they remember will be out of your control—their friends, their teachers, their private thoughts, and emotions allows each of them to live a life no one else is part of—many of their hours are spent in your presence.

MUCH OF WHAT YOUR CHILDREN REMEMBER, LEARN, AND FEEL WILL COME FROM YOU AS A PARENT. MUCH OF WHAT THEY EVENTUALLY PASS ON TO THEIR OWN CHILDREN WILL COME FROM THEIR IMPRESSIONS OF WHAT WAS IMPORTANT TO YOU.

Few things you can leave your children will endure, but memories will.

Let's look at what a regular dad can do to promote memories in his children. I read of one dad who created a rather powerful memory for each of his children. Although this man wasn't particularly wealthy, when each child graduated from high school, dad and child went on a trip to a location of the child's choice anywhere in the world.

This was obviously an elaborate memory-producer that cost a good deal of money and took a lot of time. But a special memory was produced in the mind of each child (and in the dad too, who made it to the Orient, Europe, South America, and other places with his children, one at a time).

I mention this idea, although such a thing may be out of the reach of most us, for several reasons. One is to make the point that here is a dad who is interested in having his children have experiences unique to them, that they look forward to and prepare for, and that create lifelong memories. Certainly these children feel that their dad cares about them.

A second significant point about this kind of experience is the message conveyed about how this dad views his son or daughter. Traveling this distance together indicates an equality. These are obviously two adults traveling, since a man wouldn't take a very young child on such a trip. That alone conveys a great deal to the young adult.

Another reason for mentioning this idea is to illustrate what can be done with careful planning. There is no limit if a dad wants to go to the trouble. This man's methods help us know it's worth a little effort to create memories for our children.

BUT TRADITIONS DON'T HAVE TO
BE ELABORATE IN THE LEAST.
SOME OF THE MOST MEMORABLE
ONES ARE VERY SMALL THINGS INDEED.

Since I started with an example of traveling around the world, let's go to the other end of the scale and look at very tiny incidents that become tradition in our homes and end up having significance, often unpredictably.

At the risk of your saying, "So what?", here are a few specifics at our house that I think our children will remember as traditions:

Dad's Sunday evening ritualistic drinking of his herb tea that no one else can stand.

Summer evening ice cream cones at a local fast food place.

President's day swimming at a nearby indoor/outdoor swimming resort.

Setting up dad's 35-year old electric train over Christmas vacation every year.

There are many other incidents, impressions, and events at our house, of course, just as there are at yours. The mix makes each family unique.

When you married, you combined your memories, traditions, and views of how things ought to be done with the memories, traditions, and views of your wife—another unique individual, whose background, no matter how similar, is different from yours. If this hasn't ever caused you moments of distress as you tried to figure out how on earth she could think so differently from you on certain things, you've either been married less than a week or you're in a coma. Especially do these differences come to the fore when you deal with holidays, in-laws, and raising children.

One young woman, Marie, found, when she married Jim, that it was traditional in his family for the married children to bring their families and spend every Sunday afternoon and holiday at his parents' house. This seemed fine at first and caused no obvious conflicts since Marie's parents lived too far away to visit often anyway. But, after a few months, this unspoken requirement started to grate on Marie who thought she and Jim ought to be able to stay home sometimes. She faced a key moment the next Sunday in deciding whether to mention it to her husband or not. When she did, she was surprised to find he agreed that such frequent visits were a lot of trouble and not necessary.

No confrontation with her parents-in-law was needed, since they probably had no idea that the young couple felt pressured to visit. What they intended as a strong "Welcome," had been interpreted as "You will come—now." Maria and Jim simply stayed home when they felt like it. A new tradition was evolving.

What you've done over the succeeding years since your marriage began, if you've been a successful couple, is that you have modified, mellowed, and adjusted your views to accommodate one another to some extent. Of course some things—hopefully all small matters—never quite get adjusted. Zina and I discuss every year, for example, whether Santa's presents should or shouldn't be wrapped. I say yes; she says no. (The solution, incidentally, is always the same: if they're small, they get wrapped. Those bigger than the living room couch are allowed to stay unwrapped.)

In many such cases, the two of us have *combined* our backgrounds and created new traditions. As our family grew, our traditions were broadened and adjusted even more as the children offered their input.

Children are often the impetus for starting and for keeping traditions going. Some traditions are even created in the first place by their asking about something we did the year before. By doing the thing twice in a row, it's on its way to becoming a tradition.

PART OF THE WONDER OF TRADITIONS IS THE ANTICIPATION.

By January of every year, we get out the highway guide and start talking about next summer's trips: our one big and several little ones. The anticipation is probably as important as the trips. Realizing early in our marriage the importance of providing family memories, my wife and I decided that we wanted to take family trips when our children were still young. We decided that, even if we had to camp out to be able to afford them, these memories were important enough that the trips should be made.

Think of those regular, repetitive events that create traditions just because they keep coming around. Christmas, the Fourth of July and other holidays, birthdays, vacations, Sundays, mealtimes, bedtimes, and church—all of these are regular events in our lives, and, therefore, prone to traditional ways of doing things.

One caution: partly because of the heightened expectations of emotion-laden holidays and events such as Thanksgiving and Christmas, stresses and disappointments are common. These events can be made too much of, leaving everyone expecting more than can be delivered.

LIKE ANY GOOD THING, TRADITIONS CAN BE CARRIED TOO FAR.

This happens when people feel bound to do things in certain traditional ways, leaving no freedom to change. Traditions ought not to become so firm that they can't be adjusted. Obviously, they mustn't change *too* much or they won't be traditions anymore. But the day a tradition is so set in concrete that no variation is allowed is the day that it becomes burdensome and oppressive. Traditions are made for man, not man for traditions. They must be free to evolve.

Therefore, when teenagers start to show less interest in some of those activities that families have previously done together, it's best to continue to invite but not to coerce. It's part of the letting go that a parent must learn to do.

SOME MEMORIES NEED CLARIFICATION AND DISCUSSION TO INVEST THEM WITH MEANING OR MAKE THEM UNDERSTANDABLE.

Memories such as the car wreck Matthew and I were in can be recalled and discussed in such a way that the traumatic effect can be softened, thus helping both of us to rid ourselves of the fright of the event.

Sometimes parents don't discuss deaths of loved ones or other "heavy" matters with their children because they don't want to bring up unpleasant memories. But children need to be able to discuss their fears and to see adults reconciling the realities we all need to face. Denial and suppression aren't helpful or realistic.

One of the incidental joys of shared memories is that they are often verbally passed down to those who didn't experience them. Half of my children weren't born, for example, when I did the dance in the milk, or when the big fish was caught, but even the youngest of them "remember" these events because they've heard the older children describe the events.

Often in the midst of an activity with my children a key moment will arise and I'll ask, "Twenty years from now, do you think we'll remember this day?" This has the effect of getting us all to stop and focus on what's happening at the moment. Whether or not the moment will actually be remembered is less important than that we all feel part of a family event.

Your children will be strengthened by your attention to the events and experiences that are unique to your family.

Topics For Discussion With Your Wife

1. Are there traditions that we grew up with that we would like to pass on but haven't yet made a point of?
2. Are there traditions that have evolved out of combining the heritage of the two of us? Are there some of these that still need to be sorted out and discussed?
3. Do we feel burdened by the demands some traditions make? Are there some we'd actually like to drop because they seem too restrictive of our freedom?
4. Are there memories of difficult times we feel we need to help our children sort through? What is our plan for doing so?
5. How much in agreement are we on the ideas in this chapter? Are we working together? Have we identified areas of difference, and are we able to talk about them? Are there major areas we need to discuss further at a future time?

5

Spend The Time

Two young boys were talking. One said, "Let's ask our dads to come outside and shoot baskets with us."

The other said, "Oh, my dad never does that."

"Why not?" asked the first, "Doesn't he like to shoot baskets?"

"He just never has time," was the reply.

"Why not?" asked the first. "He comes home from work the same time my dad does."

"Yeah, but he's just always busy."

"Well, what does he do?"

"Oh, I don't know, just reads the paper and stuff, and watches TV."

"Oh. Well, my dad does that too, but he still shoots baskets when I ask him."

This discussion describes a situation filled with the potential for regret. Some of us dads are just too busy to get around to the most important things. Look at the key moments missed! If we're not careful, time races by and our children move out to be on their own before we get some of the most important moments spent with them.

GIVEN A FREE CHOICE, THE TIME
WE SPEND ON SOMETHING TELLS
HOW MUCH WE VALUE OR ENJOY IT.

Of course, we don't always have a perfectly free choice. Most of us have obligations such as work and church that take a portion of our time. We need to spend time sleeping, eating, and taking care of our own needs. Our freedom to choose is also somewhat constrained by prior choices.

Yet we usually have some discretionary time. Some people think they don't have any until they look at how they spend their days and find that it isn't all structured by outside forces, after all. If we spend our "free" time reading the paper, weeding the flowers, or changing the oil—all worthy tasks, mind you—and have no time for our children, we're expressing certain values, whether we know it or not.

This isn't to say that a dad has no right to time for himself, for his spouse, for his own interests, or for chores and necessities. A dad has that right; he's a person too, and no guilt is necessary even for a certain amount of "selfish" time use.

Make no mistake about it: kids take a lot of time, and without some effort at "holding our own," parents can be devoured and sucked dry. Parenthood can be so consuming that a few parents become dependent on the requests and expectations made by their children until they have no life of their own. That's no more the ideal than is giving too little time to their family.

It may seem hard to believe when they're very young and very noisy, but relatively soon those children will be flying out of the nest, leaving us with all that quiet we thought we wanted. It will be a mixed blessing, I suspect, and there may be regrets that better use wasn't made of the time we had together.

The time we have with our children is short. How clearly I recall, years ago, overhearing other parents discussing concerns they had in raising teenagers. Our first child, Angela, was just a few weeks old at the time.

"Ah, that's a long, long time away for me," I remember thinking. I've remembered that naive thought many times. I remembered it on the day Angela became a teenager. That "long, long time" had gone by faster than I possibly could have anticipated.

Some people are always waiting for something before they get around to enjoying their children. Maybe they're working extra hard to buy a bigger house, a van, a boat, expensive trips, or annuities for retirement. Or maybe they're giving their time to keeping the house or yard in shape. These are acceptable activities in themselves.

But such parents need to be aware that life is now, and that what our children really want is time with us. Someday all parents will wake up to a quiet house, with the children all moved out. And the chance to do all those things they meant to do will be gone. Life just happens to be right now.

This isn't a book on time management, but let me just state a basic principle: organizing your time is largely a matter of attitude.

YOU'LL GENERALLY FIND TIME FOR THOSE THINGS YOU REALLY WANT TO DO.

If you think of going home after work to "free time," meaning time only for yourself, this sets up an attitude in you that labels as an intrusion any time your children demand; their demands are an interference with your "free" time. If, on the other hand, your attitude is that you are going home to *family* time, as well as personal time, you will not find your children's expectations so disruptive.

But the busy dad's standard answer to the time problem is something like this: "I can't spend much time with my children. But while the quantity is small, I make up for it in quality." I think we need to look at this idea in a little more depth.

Certainly, there are dads who are home but not really there. Between seven and eleven p.m., many of them are either in front of the TV with their eyes open or with their eyes closed. So they're not really present in any significant way. This is the quantity-over-quality group, and their problem is obvious.

But what about the quality-over-quantity group? Do they have a problem?

No one would argue that quality time isn't better than non-quality time, no matter what the quantity. That would be like arguing that a meaty, juicy hamburger isn't better than a dry, burned one just because they're the same size. That would be silly; quality is always better.

The question is whether a *lot* of quality time isn't better than a *little* quality time. It's nonsense to hope that spending two minutes in deep discussion with your boy or girl can replace hours of interaction, even if the hours are less intense than the two minutes.

CERTAINLY THE EFFORT FOR QUALITY HAS TO BE MADE. BUT DADS MUST TRY TO GET AS MUCH QUANTITY AS IS REASONABLE TOO.

Marriages often fail when too little time is spent in constructive engagement. Failure in father-child relationships occur for the same reason. People have to know each other to like each other. When too little time is spent, even if there isn't any particular animosity, there can still be estrangement because people just don't know each other.

It takes time to get to know people. But that's just what you want to do with your children, while they're still at home. Here are a few ways a regular dad can improve the quality *and* the quantity of the time he spends with his family.

1. TALK. One way to get to know your children is to talk to them, to ask their opinions, even advice. At our house, opinions on various family matters are asked. Suggestions for trips, input on rules for running the household, and advice on family purchases have been sought.

INSIGHTS DON'T SEEM TO DEPEND ON AGE, AND SOME OF THE BEST IDEAS HAVE COME FROM OUR YOUNG CHILDREN.

Asking hypothetical questions is a fun way to get to know people because such questions encourage discussion and teach the children that they're able to have views of their own. At our dinner table, we've discussed everything from what the world would be like today if America had lost the Revolutionary War to why bigger servings aren't given at school lunch. Such discussions indicate to a child that we want to hear his or her opinion and that we are listening.

Questions such as, "Which would you rather be, a pilot or a ship captain?" are also good for getting children used to thinking things through and coming up with answers. It's a safe situation in which they can practice thinking, since such opinion answers can only be "right."

Open-ended social issues, such as "What obligations does government have to take care of the disabled?" are great discussion issues for older children. Be sure to listen to their views even if they aren't as informed as yours. And be careful about giving your ideas too soon, because that will tend to tell them that they should hold back and wait for the "right" answer.

I ask about the most interesting thing that happened at school that day. This will often bring out a discussion of what was served at school lunch, but sometimes much more than that. Someone will start telling about something being studied, and we then all listen to that expert for a few minutes.

One way to involve the youngest children in family interaction is to spice up their bedtime stories by putting their own names into the story or by letting them fill in a few blanks. A beginning like, "Bre'r Rabbit came down the road and heard a sound like. . ." gives them a chance to finish the sentence and be part of the narrative. And the story is bound to be more interesting and imaginative than dad's solo effort would be.

All of these are ways to get children to express themselves and to learn confidence in doing so.

2. QUIET TIME. Time spent with children needn't always be organized into talking, traveling, playing games, or working. Just spending time in the presence of one another has great value, too.

One way we've found that works well at our house is to encourage our children to bring their homework to the dining room table after dinner. Though they're free to choose, we prefer having them together rather than hiding out in their rooms. I like the physical proximity; it feels good. I bring the newspaper, my writing, and any other paper work I may have, and several of us will spend time around the table for part of the evening. Occasionally we pop some popcorn or have a soft drink.

Sunday afternoons and evenings at our house are similar in that we encourage our children to stay home and we all seem to congregate, for at least part of the day, in the living room. Sometimes we talk; other times we read or listen to music, in our own mental worlds but still in the midst of those we love most.

THE POINT IS THAT THESE ARE
CASUAL, UNSTRUCTURED TIMES
WHEN WE'RE JUST TOGETHER.

I believe these times provide feelings of warmth and acceptance that each child feels. As for the parents, we think it's just neat to have the children around.

3. LIMIT TV. Watching TV together can be a worthwhile family experience, but not, in my opinion, for thirty hours a week. It demands too much attention to fit into the "quiet-time" type of activity already described. In excess, TV watching is just a mental babysitter, a routine time-filler, and won't contribute anything significant to family togetherness, in spite of our sitting there mesmerized together.

I don't recommend throwing out the TV but I do recommend taking control of its use. TV needs limits; it needs to know who's boss. My strongest advice is to never, never, never play it during dinner.

It may not be fashionable in many homes, but I think it best to have the children ask a parent if the TV can be turned on. Otherwise, the tube simply eats up too much time. A recent Epcot Poll indicated that one-third of American adults claim they watch four to six hours of TV a day. I don't know how they get *anything* else done. At our house, TV watching is limited.

4. USE COMMITTED TIME. Just as my bringing the newspaper to the dining room table in the evening gets the paper read without shutting out the family, there are numerous ways to "find" time for your children by involving them in whatever you are already committed to doing.

ONE SIMPLE WAY TO GET TO KNOW
CHILDREN IS TO TAKE THEM
ALONG ON ERRANDS, SHORT OR LONG.

I seldom run an errand in town without inviting a child or two to come along. This provides a chance to talk casually on the way to doing something else, at no extra "cost" in time. The same idea applies to yard work, housework, exercise and recreation time, and even to professional work.

Another way I use committed time is to take a day off on my child's birthday when possible. My work schedule has usually allowed me to do this. If school isn't in session, I stay home the whole day. If school is on, I take the child to school, then go to work, and come home early to meet him or her. This day is their's to plan.

This is committed time when I would normally be at work. Therefore, I am able to freely give that day to my child without missing it. This is precious time to a child because it's dedicated to him and he knows it can't be interrupted.

5. CHANGE THE SCENERY. Seeing children in a new environment can tell a dad a lot about them. Outdoor events like camping are excellent ways to see people as they react to their new surroundings. Different behavior is visible when the daily routine is varied by finding new scenery.

Often children who seem lazy at home take on new vitality in such a setting where the chores are perhaps more obvious and more vital and where the results of sloppy work may result in a cold dinner or a rain-soaked sleeping bag.

Coming to dad's office for part of the day, including lunch, is a popular change of scenery with my children. I'm sure it's primarily the lunch that's the attraction, but I also think it communicates an equality to be seen around the office with dad. Taking a son or daughter to the office or place of work can be fun for them but, more than that, it can be a learning experience too, helping the child learn more about the types of work available in the world.

If your work takes you out of town, take one of your children along now and then. They'll be excited about it and you'll have a chance to give individual time to that child in a new setting.

6. INDIVIDUAL TIME. As valuable as group activities with the family are in binding you together as a group, individual time is also vital. I learned this when David was perhaps six years old and he and I got to wrestling several evenings in a row. Taylor, who was about three, soon wanted in on the action. David was incensed.

"You're too little," he told Taylor.

It was a key moment and I'm not sure I handled it right. I immediately came to Taylor's rescue and pulled him into the melee.

David's interest in wrestling decreased instantly. Over the next several nights it was Taylor or I who said, "Let's rassle." David still participated but it wasn't the same.

IT TOOK ME QUITE A WHILE TO FIGURE OUT THAT IT WAS THE INDIVIDUAL ATTENTION THAT DAVID WANTED, PLUS THE FEELING OF BEING THE "BIGGEST," NOT THE WRESTLING, PER SE.

When his little brother joined in, wrestling became, for David, just another family activity, not special like it had been. Had I known what I now know about individual time, I would have found something else to replace the wrestling for David instead of being so insistent on teaching my "fairness" lesson.

A "date night" or a lunch with dad is a great way to get to know an individual child, and it gives him something to anticipate, along with a feeling of being treated in a special way.

One way of giving individual attention in the midst of a group setting is to say something like this at the dinner table: "One rainy December morning when we were living in Western Samoa, your mom woke me up to say it was time to go to the hospital."

Even when Taylor was only three or four years old, it was fun to see his eyes light up as he recognized the story of his birth, and it's been true of the others too. This focusing of attention on one of the children by the rest of us makes him or her feel special.

One last method of giving special attention to one at a time is an approach I've used at some points in my life. Without announcing it to anyone, I've considered Monday Angela's day, Tuesday David's, etc. (The number of children I have happen to just fill one week— one for each day.) On that day I try to spend a little extra time with that child.

7. FIND THEIR INTERESTS. School events, or other things that your children find important, are a great way to show interest in them. Whenever possible, I attend parent-teacher conferences with

Zina to learn of my children's work and to let them know of my interest. (Do you know your children's school and church teachers,
dad?)

One of the greatest values in scouting, as far as I'm concerned—
especially Cub Scouting—is that it provides a common task for parents and children to work on. Sitting down with a boy to do a scout
project is a great way for a dad and his son to develop common interests and to show him that his growth and learning are important.
A similar contact needs to be maintained with your daughters.

8. EQUALITY. It's important to let your children know, as they
grow up, that they are your equals, perhaps not in responsibility for
the family, but in many other ways. When David was just past his
"Santa Claus years," he asked one Christmas eve if he could stay
up and help me be Santa.

I honestly didn't like the idea at first. Maybe I didn't want him
to grow up so soon, or maybe I didn't want to let go of my exclusive
role. But in this key moment I said, "Sure," and he was thrilled to
help me fill the stockings. I sent him to bed before putting out the
other gifts so he would have some surprises the next morning too.
Nearly every year since, he's continued to help.

Our younger children have been given a small plot in the garden
to plant and take care of. I believe one reason they like this is because it indicates to them an equality and a trust.

Humor is a great equalizer. Enjoying a laugh together tells your
children that you value them and enjoy them as equals. If you can
laugh with your children and show them that life is sometimes cra-
zy and just plain silly, you will have shown them a key principle
of sane and happy living.

9. INTERVIEWS. One fine way to get to know your children is
through interviews. Sitting down once a month or so for an informal talk sets the stage for some great sharing together. An interview
is more than just a regular conversation. Setting the time in advance
seems to set the stage for an important discussion.

However, when I use the word "interview," I must be careful to
point out the informality that is the key here.

IF YOU MAKE THIS A PREACHING SESSION, GET TOO HEAVY WITH THE QUESTIONING, OR JUDGMENTAL ABOUT WHAT IS TOLD YOU, INTERVIEWS WILL ULTIMATELY FAIL.

Think of interviews as times to chat about important things, but be careful to keep the discussion open and free, the tone informal and non-judgmental, and the questions sincere but not too probing. And listen, listen, listen.

Some of my children are easy to get started talking about how they feel. Others are more difficult. In the latter case, I suggest starting them off with some questions or ideas that are general enough for them to find a response to. Here are some possibilities:

What I like best about our family is . . .

What I like best about school is . . .

When I'm alone, I like to . . .

When I'm sad, I feel like . . .

In the coming year I want to . . .

When I'm upset with a member of our family, I . . .

I'm happy when . . .

The thing I would most like to change about myself (or this family or the world) . . .

When I do something nice for someone else, I . . .

The family rule I dislike the most is . . .

When I need someone to talk to, I . . .

I believe in . . .

My greatest fear is . . .

These open-ended statements can be varied to match the age of the child. Using just a few of them will sometimes lead you into a discussion. You can make up new ones as you go.

One interview caution: It's human nature to ask "Why?" Try not to do so. Children will seldom know why they think a certain way, but the pressure of your asking can cause them to feel they have to make up something. And it's seldom important anyway.

These ideas, and others that you will come up with, can help you spend valuable time with your family. Your children won't live at home for long, and though we all hope to let them leave graciously when that time comes, we will have fewer regrets about their time with us if we build good memories of talking, working, and loving together.

(Some of the material in this chapter was originally published by the author in the June 1979 *Ensign* under the title "One to One.")

Topics For Discussion With Your Wife

1. How do we each feel about the time we spend with our children? What is our attitude about time? Do we feel pressured? Do we manage to make time for those things we really want to do?

2. How are we at enjoying our children now, as opposed to postponing finding the time until "later"?

3. How do we look at the quality vs. quantity question regarding time with our children? How can we improve either or both of these? Which of the listed items (talking, quiet time, limiting TV, using committed time, changing the scenery, individual time, finding their interests, equality, interviewing) do we want to improve on in spending time with our children?

4. How much in agreement are we on the ideas in this chapter? Are we working together? Have we identified areas of difference, and are we able to talk about them? Are there major areas we need to discuss further at a future time

6

Work Together

A common sight every afternoon in our neighborhood a few years ago was a station wagon coming slowly down the street with the rear gate down. In this opening sat an eleven or twelveyear old neighbor boy, feet dangling, lobbing newspapers into driveways as his mother drove him on his paper route. Each and every day, rain or shine, as far as we could tell, she drove while he dangled and lobbed.

She sounds like a wonderful mother, doesn't she? My children, who had to walk their own paper routes in cold or heat, rain or snow, hail or hurricane, thought so. But I wonder what was going on. This boy was healthy and able. There was no physical reason why he couldn't have walked his route, which covered only a few blocks.

Why was he driven? I don't know, but I can only guess that his mother felt she was being a good parent by doing him this daily favor.

I wouldn't presume to judge the quality of this woman's parenthood by this single act. Nor would I predict how her boy will turn out. Single acts don't usually make the difference. But I would venture to suggest that, in the long run, she was not helping her boy. And I admit to some interest in someday discovering if he grows up knowing how to work.

If you're from the American middle class, as most of us are, I suspect you're already convinced of the need to teach your offspring to work. But, except for those who live on real, working farms, whose children are already necessarily part of the team, many modern parents have trouble finding meaningful work for their children to do. In urban areas, contributions our children can make to the family in the way of work aren't always obvious. Parents in this environment sometimes spend more energy looking for ways to keep their children involved in significant work than it would take to do the work themselves. But, in either the farm or the urban setting, most dads are convinced that work is somehow good for their children. Let's stop and consider why this particular virtue seems so valuable to most of us.

Do you value knowing how to work just for the purpose of earning a living? Let's ask it this way: If you had unlimited money and knew a foolproof way for your children to inherit it after you had used all you could of it, would you still want your children to know how to work?

WOULD YOU TEACH YOUR CHILDREN TO WORK IF THEY WERE GUARANTEED TO NEVER HAVE TO EARN A LIVING?

If your answer to those questions is yes, then there must be more value in work than in just showing people how to earn a living.

At some point—or at several points—in your career as a parent, your children will likely question the value of this wonderful thing called work.

"Why do I have to clean this sink?" they will whine. "Why do I have to do everything around here?" the ingrates will moan as they become a little older. "I didn't get this wall dirty; why do I have to scrub it?" they will yelp, perhaps throwing in that most stinging of all accusations an offspring can lob at his parent: "You're not fair."

What's the answer in this key moment, dad? Why *does* your poor, weak, misunderstood little bairn have to suffer so under your cruel whip? Let's look at the possible ways you and I have probably answered these questions about work.

The first possibility, when we feel our authority is being challenged, is something like, "Do it because I told you to." But while this might suffice at a certain level, and could, if you're lucky, cut down the arguing, it isn't a direct answer as to why work is valuable. It's just a warning about not talking back.

A second answer that isn't too bad is, "You need to work so that you will learn how." This presumes that somewhere in the future, your offspring will need to take care of their own households or to earn their own living. So this answer suggests that this sink-scrubbing and dish-washing you're having them do is just for practice.

Another response: If they happen to be working for money, either for you or for someone outside the home, you might respond, "So you will learn the value of money." Therefore, this is an economics lesson you're teaching, right? You'd like your children to learn that an ice cream cone costs a half-hour's worth of their own sweat, and a record album two to four hours of hard labor.

Another answer as to why we want our little lazies to work is, "Because your parents shouldn't have to do everything." In this case we're teaching a fairness lesson: there is plenty to be done, and it isn't fair if some members of the family work while others, also able-bodied, get a free ride.

A fifth possible answer is, "Because there's just too much work for us parents to do alone." In this case, you're not teaching them to work for the future, giving an economics lesson, or teaching fairness. You're just saying, as the climber did when asked why he climbed the mountain, "Because it's there." The work is there, it needs doing, it's too much for parents to accomplish alone, and help is needed.

These are all acceptable reasons. They're all valid and "true" so far as they go. I've used them, and you probably have, too. However, there are some additional reasons I'd like to mention which I think supply deeper purposes for teaching your children to work. None of the following reasons would make much sense to the child. These are just things for dads to keep in mind.

THE MAIN REASONS FOR WORK
ALL HAVE TO DO WITH
SELF-ESTEEM IN THE CHILD.

Let me explain why I believe that. Children often tend to grow up feeling less than useful or capable. Think of how it looks from the viewpoint of a small child:

All the bigger people around me seem so much more competent. They can do magical things like unscrew fruit jar lids with their bare hands, read letters from grandma, ride bicycles without falling, and squeeze toothpaste out of tubes that are nearly flat. They can do lots of things, and I cannot. I try, but it doesn't work very well. Oh, I can do a few things; for example, I spill things, break things, ruin things, lose things, and forget where I put things. And, you know what? Everybody notices all the wrong things I do and they all tell me to be careful, stay away from their stuff, *be careful*, use both hands, BE CAREFUL, quit being so clumsy, and *BE CAREFUL!*

This monologue could be extended, but the point is probably clear: Most children, at some age, take the criticism and observations of their relative incompetence, run them through the subconscious computer of their minds, and come up feeling that they aren't worth much. In the worst cases, this feeling persists right on into adulthood. Lifelong low self-esteem is the result, negatively effecting everything these people do.

But if we're careful, and a little lucky, this feeling can be largely held at bay until the child learns, over time, that he's competent after all. And I believe that work is one of the main ways for a child to learn that he's competent and worthwhile.

Therefore, I'm convinced that one of the main values of childhood work is to teach competence and self-esteem. Here are three ways work contributes to these positive attitudes.

1. FEELING USEFUL. First, I believe that children, like adults, have to feel useful. They need to feel that they are making a contribution. It isn't enough just to be loved; people need to feel needed. Work allows them to make this contribution. Even if it's just clearing their own dishes from the table at the age of two or three, children need to feel that they're doing their share. Notice how a toddler will ask to "help mommy" or "help daddy." Self-esteem is a product of feeling needed.

CHILDREN NEED TO FEEL THAT
THEY ARE MAKING A REAL

CONTRIBUTION TO THE FAMILY.

A major way to help children grow into responsible adults is to see that they make a contribution to the family in some form. In middle-class America, real contributions to the monetary welfare of the family on the part of children aren't common. Nor is it easy for parents to find ways to make it happen. Most household chores are peripherals like carrying out the garbage. Sure, it has to be done, but if junior doesn't do it, someone else will, so it's not a big thing either way. It's necessary for a dad to find ways for his children to make contributions to the family.

Dishes, cooking, laundry, housecleaning, yard, and garden work can all be real, necessary chores that must be done on time. There is no reason why children shouldn't share in these duties. Responsibility isn't *caught* by watching parents work; it's *taught* by making assignments and expecting results. A child of any age from toddler on up can help with appropriate household chores. And some of those chores can be significant learning experiences involving planning and thinking things through, as in the following example:

Lisa was twelve when her parents proposed that she handle the family food preparations for a month. With her mother's guidance, she planned the month's menus, bought the groceries, and prepared all the meals. She had to ask for help with some things, but no adult interfered without Lisa's requesting aid.

The results weren't always professional. When did the first key moment arise, do you suppose? That's right, the first time dad's favorite casserole was a little dry. But, fortunately for Lisa, dad recognized that this was a key moment and handled it correctly by keeping his mouth filled with casserole instead of commentary.

Lisa herself commented that the casserole hadn't come out right, to which dad replied it was the best casserole he'd had all day. No one even complained when the potatoes were undercooked the first time and the roast a little burned. Learning occurred and Lisa went away from the experience much more confident of her abilities.

And guess who got the assignment the next month? Pete, Lisa's fourteen-year old brother. Cooking skills aren't just for women these days. My own boys have learned at nine or ten years of age to make delicious rolls for Sunday dinner that are just as good as their mother makes, which is a compliment to her, since it was she who taught the boys.

2. LEARNING TO ACHIEVE. Work teaches children how to achieve, to do things, to be successful.

SELF-ESTEEM IS INCREASED IN CHILDREN WHEN THEY ACHIEVE AND SUCCEED.

Children soon see that the way to be one of those competent older people they're surrounded by is to learn to do things. The appropriate tasks assigned children teach them they can succeed. When they learn how capable they are in these jobs, they get a self-esteem boost which effects everything they do in their lives from that point.

When my boys have done most of the work on their Pinewood racers for Cub Scouts, and I've praised them for it, I've seen the glow of pride in their eyes whether or not they win the race. I've known some dads who build the whole car for their boys on the premise that a nine-year-old can't do it right. Wrong. Maybe dad can do it better, but what's the point of the whole event? Is it to help dad with his self-esteem? With just a little help in planning, sawing, and drilling, a nine-year-old can do a great job.

3. HAPPINESS. Third, there's a not surprising result of better self-esteem and feelings of competence in young people who learn to work.

A LONG-TERM UNIVERSITY STUDY SHOWED THAT YOUTH WHO WORKED BECAME HAPPIER ADULTS THAN THOSE WHO DIDN'T WORK.

Researchers agree that work is the prime childhood variable in a survey started in the 1940's which studied 456 teen-age boys who have now grown to middle-age. Those who worked as youth, even if just at simple household chores, have, by now, earned more money, lived longer, had better marriages, and had closer relationships with their own children. Most significantly, they rated themselves far happier than did those who said they had no work responsibilities as youth.

Psychologists interpret these results this way: the confidence and self-esteem gained through these work experiences carried over into adult life. Since these boys felt worthwhile and projected confidence, others felt the same way about them, and their lives were altered in measurable, positive ways, bringing them greater happiness in the long run. It shouldn't surprise us that a better self-concept results in a more satisfied, happier person.

So we need to have our children learn to work for more reasons than just the standard ones—learning to work for the future, learning the value of money, learning fairness, and helping get the job done. They also need to work so that they will feel like contributors, become achievers, and go on to greater happiness.

Personally, therefore, I would answer the earlier question about whether I would have my children learn to work even if they would never need the money, this way: "Absolutely. They're working for their own growth and happiness."

Now, let's talk about some cautions in teaching our children to work. Just as I thought it odd parenting for the woman in our neighborhood to drive her boy on his paper route every day, there may be those who have similarly shaken their heads at the Woods' parenting as they've seen our children out in the rain, snow, or typhoon delivering their papers. For years, our children shared a twice-weekly afternoon paper delivery, and only very, very rarely—when someone was sick or had to hurry to some evening activity at school or church—did they have any parental help.

Of course, I happen to think it was good for them. I hope it was. But at times even I wondered if it wasn't too much.

WORK CAN BE OVERDONE.
WHILE IT'S BASIC,
IT ISN'T EVERYTHING.

If you've loaded your child down with guilt when he isn't working, so that he feels that anything besides work is wasting time, beware. Some who were great workers in their youth have grown up to be the laziest types. At some point it all became drudgery, or they felt they were being taken advantage of, or that they had no free choice, and they concluded that life had to hold more than that. So they went too far the other way in rejecting work.

I've seen children who I think had adult work responsibilities thrust on them at too early an age. They missed out on the parties, friends, and normal activities of childhood. Though this isn't the norm in modern middle-class America—quite the contrary—it's still a real danger. Dads need to be careful of this. Let your kids still be kids.

IT'S EASY TO BEGIN TREATING CHILDREN LIKE SLAVES.

They're always there, they're anxious to help (at first), and their quick little legs make running upstairs to get dad his gloves or running next door to borrow a can of peas look like fun. And often it is fun for them, but enough can quickly turn to too much. Be careful of too many of these nagging requests.

The very accessibility of children tends to make parents assume that their activities are less important than their own. But children need some time to carry on with what they're doing, even if it's "only" playing. Perhaps the best guideline is to feel free to call on your child, but no more often than you would call on an adult.

Just as you, dad, like to feel you've finished your work for the day or the week, children like to feel they've done their jobs and have some free time, too. Too much calling on them to do additional things can be irritating and can communicate to them that they're only of worth when they're serving you.

Young people value their independence and free time just as you do. If you become a nag, you will make them dislike being around you.

An easy method of removing yourself from the role of nag is to create, with the help of your children, a chore chart. With such a chart, the assignments are already written down and no nagging is necessary. In our house, chore assignments rotate on a monthly basis. The children were in on that decision as well as the question of what to put on the chart, and how to divide the chores so that

the workload was evenly distributed between the rotating assignments.

While we occasionally have to go to the chart and launch a man-
hunt for the youngster assigned a specific job that needs doing at
the moment, for the most part the children keep track of their own
assignments. This keeps us parents out of the role of slave drivers.

We had no chore chart when I was growing up. But from the time
I was six years old until I was fourteen, when we lived on a small
farm, I knew my regular daily chores. One of my main jobs in the
summer was to keep the garden weeded, and it was a big one (though
when I visited the old place in recent years, the garden area had
unaccountably shrunk in size from the vast acreage of my memory).

My mom often encouraged me to be wise and get up early to get
my hoeing done before the heat of the day was upon me. But wise
I seldom was. I couldn't quite manage to get up, and would get around
to my task at ten or eleven o'clock, just as the sun was reaching its
full, blazing glory. Mom could have gotten me up, but it never occurred to me to suppose that she should. I would probably have
resented it greatly. Slave driver she was not. She left it to me.

Besides nagging, there's another danger to be avoided in helping
young people learn to work. It's the danger of keeping yourself and
your family under constant pressure to "get all our work done" before anything else. The problem is that, in running a household, especially with a yard, garden, and house to take care of, it *never* all
gets done.

SOME PEOPLE NEVER TAKE BREAKS OR VACATIONS BECAUSE THEY ALWAYS HAVE TOO MUCH TO DO.

This is cruel and unusual punishment to your children as well as
to yourself. Life is now, remember? If you don't balance work with
leisure, you may find that life has passed you by, and, in addition,
that you have irreparably damaged your child's view of work, making it endless drudgery in his mind.

Work has to have two elements to be bearable: a purpose and an
ending point. If you're a Type-A, "driven" type of personality, con-

stantly worrying about all the things you have to do and living under the illusion that you will first "get all the work done" and then take a rest, try not to pass this fallacy on to your children.

Leisure sometimes takes a bad rap in our American Puritan ethic. Of course, like anything else, it can be overdone, if that's what you're worried about, and of course, it has to be earned. But it should have a valuable place in your life, and in the life of your children. Balance the two, and teach your children the value of well-earned leisure.

Now, a word about rewards. We've been told many times that the psychological motivation of virtually everything we do is an anticipated reward in some form. Whether we accept that view fully or not, it's clear that much that we do brings us rewards, either visible or invisible.

The nature of the reward can vary greatly. A reward for an adult may be the paycheck at the end of the month or, further down the line, a secure retirement or, even further, a good place in heaven. The reward may sometimes be more subtle and internal, such as a good feeling of having helped someone, done one's duty, or completed a task.

Young people also work for rewards. Theirs, too, may be external (money, praise), or internal (a good feeling), but their rewards won't be too different from your own.

In the fourth grade, our Geneal beat her teacher on a timed math page after challenging her nearly every day for three or four weeks. Miss Youd's promised milk shake was the supposed external reward Geneal was working for, but I think it actually had more to do with the internal motivation she felt to meet the challenge and show she could do it.

The ideal would probably be for a child to do his work for the good feeling he gets from it. That's the long-term goal. But a little external reward along the way—such as praise—sure can't hurt anything either and it's one of the best things a regular dad can give.

PRAISE FROM DAD FOR DOING A GOOD JOB IS ONE OF THE GREATEST MOTIVATORS THERE IS.

Since money is one of most obvious external motivators, and since it ties in rather closely to work, let's look at money under the three headings of bribes, wages, and allowances.

1. BRIBES. These are no good. They communicate to the child that work is rotten, but if you'll just do it, you'll get an ice cream cone. An occasional promise of future reward (a bribe), in the form of a challenge for speed or extra quality to show a child what he can do if he really tries, makes more sense than a bribe for just doing the job. You may teach something you didn't want to teach if you offer bribes to get those things done a child ought to be assigned anyway.

2. WAGES. A bribe isn't the same as wages. You might conceivably pay your child for some of the work he does, though not for those things that are his expected contribution to the family. Pay can be given for extra jobs that you might negotiate with your child. Your children should know that they can earn extra money from you when they need it, which teaches them initiative and negotiation skills.

One way to look at extra pay for extra work is this: if you would pay an outsider to do it, consider paying your own child. When we've gone out to PTA meetings or church activities, as part of our obligations as parents, we haven't generally paid our older children to baby sit. When we've gone to a movie, we normally have.

3. ALLOWANCES. Wages paid for specific tasks should be separate from allowances. Nearly all child-rearing experts recommend that a child get an allowance just for being. An allowance is a way of saying that this child is a part of our family and needs a little money to spend and to learn to manage.

I would not tie the allowance to chores or to quality of chores, unless you want to do it in a very loose way as a motivator for getting things done on time, such as, "Every week, when the Saturday chores are done, you can collect your allowance." This means the allowance could be given on the next Monday if that's when "Saturday's" chores get done. (If you don't like Saturday's chores not getting done until Monday, find another enforcer besides allowance.)

Handling money is a skill you need to help your children practice. From the day our children earned their first money, or received their first allowance, they've been shown how to pay their church offerings, then divide the rest equally into spending and savings. Before they were old enough to really miss it, therefore, half of their money went into their bank accounts. By the time they were adolescents, our children had sizable amounts they were proud of.

If you wait until a child is sixteen years old before suggesting he save half of his money, you will meet an argument head on. By then he knows lots of things he'd like to buy. Start early and savings will be a habit.

Before leaving the subject of rewards, look at this list of motivators found to be effective in the work place. These are the things adults say they work for on the job. They may not differ too much from what our own children want.

1. Recognition
2. Tangible rewards (more money or benefits)
3. Changes in job tasks for variety
4. Self-management and decisionmaking opportunities
5. Increased status
6. Feedback on quality of work
7. Breaks and privileges, time for personal activities
8. Social activities (job-related parties)
9. Relief from some duties
10. Improved office or environment

(From the "National Society for Performance and Instruction Journal," Washington, D.C., NSPI, July 1978)

I find it interesting that so many of the things adults find motivating apply so obviously to children. If we employ people, we're interested in motivating them to do their best work. They won't work for nothing. Let's not expect young people to work for "nothing" either.

At the age of two, your child will be eager to help you. It's never too early. How you handle his interest is a key moment, because you will convey something about your feelings for your child's abilities at this moment.

A young child loves to tag along and "help" daddy, long before the age of being able to make a real contribution. Find something for him to do. Just don't demand too much. Expect him to work only when you're right beside him, helping.

Working *with* a child of any age is an excellent way to show him how to do a job and to make it more fun. You're also teaching lessons in teamwork and cooperation, which are by-products of learning to work.

AVOID CONVEYING TO YOUR YOUNG CHILD WHO IS TRYING HIS BEST THAT HIS WORK ISN'T GOOD ENOUGH.

This message will be a deadly killer of that child's interest in work. If you have to re-wash the bathroom mirror after your four-year-old washed it, don't let him know.

If you demand that your four-year old clean the bathtub as well as you do, you're going to set him—and you—up for frustration. On the other hand, a fifteen-year old ought to be held to that standard and can be sent back to fix sloppy work. At this point, the best way to be sure of communicating the right way to do the job is on hands and knees, to show the child exactly what you expect. Be sure you are merely demanding as good a job as you would do, not a better one. Be careful, too, to allow your creative offspring some leeway in *how* the job is done, as long as the results are good.

In this day and age, dad, I would make a point of having boys as well as girls learn household chores. The days have passed when women alone did all the housework, and you will handicap your son if you don't insist that he learn to vacuum, clean bathrooms, do laundry, change diapers, and cook.

A job outside the home is the way a child can apply those work skills you've been trying to teach. Folding and delivering the twice-weekly papers that were brought to our house every Wednesday and Saturday for ten years taught our children more about punctuality and consistency than we could have hoped to do in the same number (one thousand and forty) of twice-weekly lectures.

When a woman in our neighborhood was in our house one day and saw our daughter, Angela, then fourteen, doing her assigned housework, she hired her to do some spring cleaning. Soon the word spread that Angela was a girl who knew how to work. She was offered as many jobs as she could handle while still in school. She worked for several people, including one who used her every Saturday morning for a year or so, before taking a part-time job at a fast foods establishment.

Angela didn't really like the housework, but she liked the money well enough. Her employers uniformly praised her for her work, and Angela's self-esteem benefited as well as her pocketbook. Incidentally, she got the fast foods job because the manager lived in the neighborhood and had heard good things about her diligence in the housecleaning field.

If you can teach your children how to work, they will be ahead of many of their peers who haven't been taught that the world is literally waiting for those who know how to apply themselves to a task.

Topics For Discussion With Your Wife

1. How do we feel about work ourselves? How much are we working for the "right" reasons? How much does our work effect our own self-esteem?

2. How do we feel about what we've taught our children about work? What are our reasons for wanting them to learn to work?

3. How could we improve the self-esteem of our children through work? Through praise?

4. How about the work load our children carry? Is it too light? Too heavy? Properly adjusted according to age and ability? Are the tasks clear to everyone?

5. Are we naggers? Do our children perceive us as naggers? Or have we arranged for them to know their chores and assignments and to carry them out on their own?

6. Do we both feel good about how breaks, vacations, and leisure are handled at our house? Is it clear to all family members that work will be balanced by leisure?

7. Do we feel good about how allowances and extra pay are handled?

8. Have we found ways for our children to contribute to the family in significant ways?

9. How much in agreement are we on the ideas in this chapter? Are we working together? Have we identified areas of difference, and are we able to talk about them? Are there major areas we need to discuss further at a future time?

7

The Home is a Refuge

It may sound old-fashioned, even trite, and a little silly, but your home should be a refuge for your children. Though I am not a hermit, or one who wants to teach my children to escape from life, I do believe the world offers a great deal of stress at times, especially to children, from which temporary relief is needed.

I'm not talking about muggings and traffic accidents. I'm talking about pressures to perform, conform, and achieve. The world can be a stressful place, but I don't want my children to fear entering that world. I just want to help them get ready for that entrance. In this and the next chapter, we'll look at how the home can be a temporary port for refitting before sailing back into the storm.

Most of us, by the time we're adults, are able to shut out the world to some extent, to create our own refuge, as it were, by ignoring certain comments and events, and retreating, at least for part of the day, behind mental defenses of our own making. Though there are limits to that effort, this defense-making is still a valuable skill that we use to more fully control our lives and to provide peace and sanity. Children, on the other hand, are less able to do that.

CHILDREN ARE MORE AT THE MERCY OF WHAT THE WORLD DISHES OUT.

They're vulnerable, inexperienced, and less skilled at thinking through solutions to problems. They often don't perceive that there is a way out. They just assume that they have to take what comes.

As an example, suppose you hire a babysitter that somehow isn't impressive to you. As an adult, you have the option to not hire him or her again. But what if your small child feels some concern, which he probably can't verbalize, about the sitter? Unless he throws a fit, you aren't even aware of the problem, so nothing changes. Even if he could state his concerns, you might likely treat them as whimsical and immature. Your young child's remonstrances probably wouldn't cause you to replace the babysitter, unless you also perceived the problem. A child just doesn't have the control that an adult has over his environment.

Let's take a peek at the world through a child's eyes, say that of an eight-year-old we'll call Tim. At school, his teacher this year seems busy, unfriendly, strict, and demanding. Even when Tim tries to do his best work, Miss Young finds his handwriting sloppy, his spelling lousy, his thinking unoriginal. Tim notices that many of his classmates do better in most subjects, read aloud better, and get more "smiley faces" on their returned work. He feels that he's doing his best and doesn't know how to do better, and he's started to wonder if he's just plain dumb.

Even recess isn't what it used to be. Tim isn't the best at any game or sport. He enjoys playing, but less this year than last, because some of the boys are now bigger than he is and they get together on one team and always win. He's never chosen for that team and he's decided he's just not very athletic, so he doesn't try very hard anymore.

Tim has friends, but no one who is really a good buddy since Tom, his best friend since kindergarten, moved away last spring. He misses having a close friend to laugh and talk with.

He's not unhappy at school, but he clearly doesn't enjoy it like he used to. He doesn't feel like he quite fits in anymore, and he doesn't know what the problem is.

After school each Wednesday, Tim goes straight to Mrs. Horsley's house for his piano lesson. Mrs. Horsley tells him every week that he isn't living up to his potential. She says he has good ability, but he just isn't practicing enough. He knows she's right, but he's not very interested. He doesn't like to practice, so he doesn't work very hard at it. But he feels he s failing his teacher, and this makes him feel guilty, so he finds himself making up silly excuses for Mrs. Horsley each week.

This list could be lengthened by mentioning other areas of Tim's life where he feels stressed, but it's clear by now that Tim is probably a pretty normal eight-year-old with an average number of pressures on him. I don't mean to portray him as having an excessive number of pressures; he's about average.

Many children are much worse off than Tim in the pressures they face. If we wanted to portray him as *above* average in the pressures he faces, we could have people making fun of him because of less than stylish clothing, crooked teeth, a lisp, or anything else that makes him stand out in the wrong way. Children can be among the most vicious creatures on earth, and without adult instruction, their tolerance for those who are different is not very great.

Of course, many of Tim's pressures could be lessened by his "growing up" and accepting that that's how life is, that there will always be pressures, that many of these things he's worried about don't matter anyway. Well, growing up is just what Tim will eventually do. But that takes time, and Tim is only eight. At the moment, he just feels the pressure.

Tim doesn't need someone to take away the pressures; they really are part of life, and he does need to learn to face them. But he needs time, understanding, and a place of temporary relief, a "time-out" corner—he needs a refuge. And he needs your attention, dad, in a number of key moments.

The kinds of problems I've portrayed Tim as having aren't the same kinds we all face with an occasional "bad day." Though there are adults who have intolerable situations, for most of us our bad days are infrequent enough that we can weather them. If not, we can usually find ways to alter our circumstances by talking to the boss or our spouse about the problem, or by taking some other action to better our situation. As adults, we're much more likely to have ways of handling our environment.

The pressures Tim feels, however, whether they originate in his own mind or in the real world, are worse in two ways: first, they're constant, and, second, he sees no hope, no way around them. These two deadly components are the stuff of which mental time bombs are made.

WITH NO RELIEF, AND NO APPARENT WAY OUT, EXCESSIVE STRESSES CAN LOWER A CHILD'S SELF-ESTEEM AND THEREBY DIMINISH HIS CHANCES FOR SUCCESS IN THE WORLD.

Just because Tim is "only average" in the number of tensions he feels, and just because he's "only eight" and will surely grow out of these problems, and just because almost everybody has felt similar pressure at times, doesn't mean Tim doesn't face a real problem. Although it's common, it's still important, and a dad can do something about it.

If Tim were your boy, what would you do? Over-reaction isn't the answer. Yanking a child out of school to teach him at home isn't a good long-term solution. That's over-protection. Someday, he's going to have to face the world. (Though there may be significant justifications for teaching children at home, this isn't one of them.) Unfortunately, what the over-reactive approach does is add to the stress by giving the child the message that there's something wrong with him after all, because he needed to be singled out and kept home.

Without withdrawing your child from real life, there are two major approaches that could be taken. One is to try to *control* or *alter* the externals: to march over to the school and straighten those people out, perhaps with a cat-o-nine-tails. The other is to teach your child to *handle* the situation through internal control, to help your child develop attitudes and skills to carry him through the problem.

Both of these approaches have value, although the latter is obviously more within your control and has the potential of teaching permanent skills that will transfer to many situations in your child's life.

Not that a visit to the school might not be beneficial. It may well be worth a talk *with*—not *to*—the teacher to point out how you think your child is feeling. You're likely to gain some insights by hearing the teacher's observations. Together you may be able to work out some methods to improve your child's situation at school. These may include extra attention by the teacher or after school tutoring—from yourself at home, from the teacher after school, or from a hired tutor.

ANY APPROACH YOU TAKE NEEDS TO BE KEPT LOW-KEY SO THAT YOUR CHILD DOESN'T PERCEIVE HIMSELF AS HAVING MORE PROBLEMS THAN HE ACTUALLY HAS.

A child will interpret any suggestions that he needs help as meaning that he's dumb, unless you explain what you are up to. It's a good opportunity for a discussion about how we all need help on various things at different points in our lives.

Be careful, too, about interceding in the child's homework problems too directly. Nearly all educators recommend leaving homework a matter between child and teacher. Especially stay away from nagging and pestering about whether the work is done. It just isn't your problem. And the danger is that your child can make homework a lever to hurt you, when he wants to rebel, thereby hurting himself.

However, here are a few things you can do in regard to homework:

Regular contact with teachers to let them know of your interest is helpful.

Let your child know of your interest by asking about his homework so he knows that you are interested in his success.

Let him know that you are available to help if he needs it.

Also provide quiet time, space, and opportunity at home for the work to be done.

These are ways to improve the external situation.

Now, as to the internals—the things you could offer your child to carry him through this, as well as future, situations. Here are a few possibilities:

1. UNDERSTANDING. A child has such limited experience in the world that he usually doesn't realize how common his feelings are. He tends to assume that he is the only one with these problems. Your key moment, dad, comes in understanding how your child sees his situation, and in letting him know you understand. A dad's telling his child that he went through similar things can be very helpful in letting him know that he can make it, too.

True understanding can only come about through listening, probing a little, and describing for your child how you think he feels,
if he's unable to say it himself.

ACCESSIBILITY AND AN INTEREST IN
REALLY LISTENING ARE THE MAIN THINGS.

But you mustn't try talking your child out of the feelings. The feelings are real. Your job is to help him to recognize that similar feelings of inadequacy exist in most people at certain times in their lives,
even in adults. His pain may still be there, but it's more easily handled if he knows it's shared by others.

Give less advice than attention. And listen.

2. COPING SKILLS. A dad can teach a child a great deal about
learning to cope. One coping skill is humor. If your child can laugh
at some aspect of the situation, he will have found a life-long coping
key.

A second coping skill is perspective. It's hard for a child to see
the big picture, but it's worth discussing. I don't mean that he should
learn to shrug everything off and pretend not to care; this is a sham.
But if he can gain perspective and see that some things just don't
matter much, he will be better off. One way to help a child do this
is to remind him of things that were important to him when he was
"little," and help him see how meaningless they seem now that he
is bigger. This can help him see that some of the things he's now
worried about won't matter much in a year or two.

Another coping skill is acceptance. A young person has to learn
to accept some things the way they are. This is a challenge because
in our culture we're taught that, if we try hard enough, we can do
anything. But a dad has to help his child count the cost. Some things
just aren't worth it, in terms of the effort required. Help him learn
that life is a series of choices about where he will spend his time
and energy. He can't do all things, nor can he be good at all things.

A child needs to know that you accept him, and that his less-than-
perfect life doesn't make you think less of him. While you always
want him to improve and learn more and do greater things, he must
know that you accept him just as he is.

AN ADDITIONAL WAY TO TEACH COPING IS TO POINT OUT THAT LIFE ISN'T A COMPETITION.

A child can learn to let others be good at some things while he's good at others. He doesn't have to be the best in everything, or even in anything.

3. COMPENSATORS. Help your child identify the things he can do well. This is a chance to show him that the things he really works at—if in perspective they're still worth the time and effort—can be achieved. If it's important to him to pitch a baseball harder and straighter, practice and instruction are bound to help. (He may need a patient catcher, dad, so dig out the old mitt.)

When I was in elementary school, we didn't play much soccer at recess, but every spring, we would play a few games before the softball season began in earnest. I still remember one play in one of those games after more than thirty years. Why? Because I was the hero. As goalie, I uncharacteristically threw myself into stopping a fast kick that was certain to score, and I blocked it. I was the team star, an unusual thing for a boy who liked to play but wasn't very good at athletics.

HELP YOUR CHILD RECOGNIZE AND REMEMBER SIMILAR EVENTS THAT REMIND HIM THAT HE'S CAPABLE, EVEN IF YOU HAVE TO STRETCH BACK TO HIS BABYHOOD.

Perhaps he was the first in your family to eat his baby food without throwing the spoon at the cat. Whatever it is that he is or was good at, remind your child of it. The message is that he is not a failure, after all.

Another compensator is knowledge. If you can supply your child with information or refer him to a source on a subject he's expressed interest in, he may become the center of attention in his circle when it comes to that subject. Arranging with the teacher to let him do a report to the class on a subject of his interest will allow him to be publicly recognized as an expert.

4. PATIENCE. A child must learn to give it time. Time heals many wounds, and, in a child, a few weeks is sometimes enough. For instance, if a child doesn't feel competent at the football games that are played at recess in the fall, a few weeks will bring cold weather and a change in games. Patience is a virtue your child can benefit from learning.

Time will also bring greater growth in physical and mental abilities. How many "slow starters" have gone on to excel later in life? Pointing this out to your child this will help him see that there is hope.

Again, as in so many topics dealing with raising children, we end up really talking about self-esteem. If you can supply your child with a good concept of himself, so many other problems will be minimized.

A STUDY BY FORMER UNIVERSITY OF CALIFORNIA PROFESSOR, STANLEY COOPERSMITH, FOUND THAT SELF-ESTEEM DEPENDED ON THREE FACTORS FROM THE HOME: LOVE, FIRM GUIDELINES, AND DEMOCRACY OR OPENNESS.

If you can provide the love in the form of warmth and acceptance, the firm guidelines in the form of consistency and clear limits, and the democracy and openness by involving all family members in family decisions and accepting their views, you will help your children become more confident and ready to face the world.

Our job, dad, is to stand with our children against the world and provide for them a place to adjust and recoup, but then to gently nudge them back out there, not to let them use the home as a permanent hideout. We will do a great disservice if we teach our children to come running home to stay. But the home needs to be established as the place that's always there, a place of refuge where children (and adults) feel welcome to come and gather strength.

Topics For Discussion With Your Wife

1. How do we feel about our home as a refuge? Have we consciously made it a place where our children can come to get recharged? Do we think they see it that way?

2. How would we evaluate our children in the pressures they feel outside the home, both in the strength of the pressures and in the way they handle them?

3. Are there ways we feel we can help our children with pressures they are facing at the moment? Identify the external and the internal things we could help with.

4. How could we better let our children know that the feelings they have are common to most people? Which experiences from our own youth could we share that might help them?

5. What coping skills could we help our children with?

6. What compensating strengths might we point out to each child that would help him know that he is capable?

7. How do we rate our home on the three Coopersmith factors relating to self-esteem? What can be done to improve any of the three that need strengthening?

8. How much in agreement are we on the ideas in this chapter? Are we working together? Have we identified areas of difference, and are we able to talk about them? Are there major areas we need to discuss further at a future time?

8

Reduce The Demands

Remember Tim from chapter 7, the average eight-year-old with the average number of pressures at school? In this chapter, we want to see what happens when Tim gets home.

As he walks in the door, mom asks him why he's late again. It turns out that he has taken some new paths across the snow on a few neighbors' lawns, and is ten minutes behind schedule. But mom wants to run an errand in town and has been anxiously waiting for Tim to get home to watch his little brother who's having his nap. Tim wants to go downstairs and watch "Get Smart" on the afternoon reruns, but mom says he can't, because with his brother asleep, he needs to stay upstairs to hear when baby brother wakes up. Mom will be back in an hour.

Tim decides to work on the model airplane he's been building since Christmas. He gets his supplies and takes them to the dining room table. But things don't go just right. Let's abbreviate this story by pointing out just some of the things that can go wrong in the next hour: just as Tim is gluing the model, the phone rings and, while he answers it, plastic cement leaks from the tube onto mom's lace tablecloth. Tim's bigger sister gets home from junior high, finds the door locked—Tim's mom has locked it as she left on her errand— and impatiently rings the doorbell three times. Tim is in the middle of gluing and can't come at the moment. When he finally goes to the door, sister accuses him of trying to keep her out—not a bad idea, he thinks, but not true, in this case. The doorbell awakens the baby, who wakes up fussy, which mom later blames on Tim.

Baby needs a diaper change, but big sister goes to her room and Tim is in the middle of his gluing right now. By the time mom gets home, baby *really* needs a diaper change. Mom asks Tim why he can't take care of these little things she asks him to do. She even accuses of him of having gone to watch TV in spite of her instructions—until she discovers the tablecloth glued to the table.

All of this takes place in the first hour Tim is home from school on what is perhaps a fairly typical day in the life of an eight-year-old. Maybe these are just common things that happen to every child. Perhaps you and I went through them and came out fine. But the list of pressures on Tim could easily be lengthened.

What happens when dad gets home and finds that Tim didn't think to shovel the new snow off the walk? What about big sister's accusations that Tim wouldn't let her in? What about mom's concern that the baby didn't get enough nap time? And what about the tablecloth?

Well, let's not overdo it, but just keep in mind that the view from Tim's eyes might be that he really can't do anything right. It isn't hard to paint a picture of childhood where nagging, correcting, judging, disagreeing, blaming, shaming, preaching, ridiculing, threatening, belittling, labeling, accusing, and comparing are the norms.

Are you sure, dad, that you don't come across in these ways to your children? (I didn't ask if you *are* this way—of course you aren't—but whether you're sure you don't *come across* this way to your children.)

Do you really accept your child? And does he know it? Are you constantly straightening him out? Oh, of course, it's for his own good. But it's still pressure. And does he perceive that it's for his own good?

CAN YOUR CHILD DISCERN BETWEEN THE NAGGING, PREACHING, AND CORRECTING YOU DO BECAUSE YOU LOVE HIM AND WHAT YOU MIGHT SOUND LIKE IF YOU DIDN'T LOVE HIM?

How much needless pressure do you add to your child's life by demanding that he do things your way, respond as you think he should, and just generally be perfect in all things?

"But," you say, "Many a child has lived through this. It's just part of growing up." Maybe this is the normal way parents act and the normal way children perceive them. All of us probably remember feeling nagged and unloved at times, in spite of our knowing—most of the time—that our parents really loved us. But just because we lived through similar feelings doesn't make that the best way to raise a child.

Not to blame your parents or mine, but consider this: Who knows but what we would be better people today if we had been handled differently in a few "small" matters? Isn't it worth a little effort to try to examine those areas where we may be less than perfect parents, or can we just shrug off any mistakes we make with, "That's the way everybody is"? Maybe the "natural man" isn't as good a dad as he could be if he tried a little harder.

We get better at our task as a dad if we try to see things from the point of view of the child. Notice in the case of Tim that he really didn't do anything so wrong, did he? Oh, he wasn't as careful as he might have been with the glue, but most of the things he was blamed for were clearly not his fault.

All of this is to illustrate a fairly "average" situation, not one of abuse or intense emotional pressure. Some children face much more serious difficulties than these.

THERE ARE SOME RATHER HEAVY DEMANDS ON EVEN THE AVERAGE CHILD.

In the last chapter, we talked of peer and school stresses primarily. In this chapter, we'll look at societal and parental pressures.

Our present society causes young people to grow up faster than they did in recent decades. Before the Renaissance, however, children had to grow up even faster. They were thought of as short adults, meaning that they were not seen as needing years of tending before they were adults. They were expected to work, contribute to the family (even through very early marriages, if that brought benefit to the family), and to grow up very fast.

By the nineteenth century, this situation had changed somewhat in that western Europe had achieved a living standard requiring, in the rising middle class, much less need for labor from children. The ideal soon turned toward a longer childhood and a recognition that, psychologically, children aren't just short adults.

In Victorian England, at least for certain social classes, childhood had become a distinct, lengthened period, and it's that ideal that has influenced American life. In this country, by the middle of the 20th century, this idea was being carried to such extremes that a child could remain a dependent in some households for as long as he wanted.

This change in viewpoint had nothing to do with length of time needed to achieve physical, mental, or emotional maturity, but generally had to do with career preparation. If this extreme meant parental support all the way through specialized professional training, a down payment on a house or, in a few cases, a grand tour of Europe after college graduation, parents who could afford it often felt obligated to provide such aid. Some "kids" were thirty-five years old and married, with families of their own, before they cut the apron strings—at least the financial ones. Though this is not the norm, neither is it all that uncommon among several people I know today.

Though many of us would agree that this idea of perpetual support can easily go too far, most American parents feel an obligation to their children at least into their early twenties. This is a far cry from the pre-Renaissance view that a girl should marry at thirteen if such a marriage could bring her family a good dowry or other advantages.

A few people today say there is no obvious need for our current view of lengthened childhood; most others, that this is a hallmark of civilization. A middle view is probably realistic. Clearly childhood shouldn't be rushed; a twelve-year-old should not have the same responsibilities as an adult. We have a chance to produce better adults when there isn't the rush to grow up.

On the other hand, I've seen 23-year-olds who were a long way from being expected to take on life; they're not only financially dependent, but immature in their decision-making ability, never having had to face up to life. To me, this is far from the ideal. Indeed, I believe these people have been harmed by the coddling they've received.

IT'S A CHALLENGE FOR A DAD TO KNOW WHEN TO KICK HIS FLOCK OUT OF THE NEST.

Though there's no "right" answer, it's an important question, worth consideration, and it's a question that primarily should be decided by the parents, not by the children. I believe that one of the major roles we play as dads is in helping our children assume appropriate, gradually increasing responsibility while still enjoying the innocence of youth and the protection of our homes until the day comes when they can, should, and must, stand on their own.

Ironically, in a era when dependency is prolonged, there is an intensity about growing up in modern America that is a product of only the last few decades. In a swing toward the trend of the pre-Renaissance world, children are rushed into growing up—not for the earlier need to contribute to the family, and not from parental pressure—but from peer pressure.

Look at the evidence. On TV many of the child stars are precocious mini-adults, who act mature for their ages, giving witty, smart, "adult" answers. I've noticed more than one comedy show where the lines delivered by the youngsters are essentially the same type as those delivered by adults. The writers make no significant age differentiation in the dialogue, and even purposely play on the humorous elements in having adult dialogue come from the mouths of babes.

Children's clothing, which used to have its own style, is now copied from adult styles. None of us may miss short pants and pinafores, nor demand that fashion never change, but the present effect is that our youth are expected to *look* grown up quicker. Pierced ears, nail polish for preschoolers, even designer bibs, may be nothing more than fun, but they also reflect a way of looking at youth that moves them faster into the adult current. Little girl beauty pageants are fairly common. One wonders whether it's the little girls or their parents who benefit the most from such events.

Sports activities, organized by adults, are a lot more "professional" than in the days of sandlot baseball. Immaculate uniforms, no-miss twice-a-day practices (even to the point of pressuring families to leave Johnnie home from summer vacation trips), team cuts, recruitment, playoffs, championships, trophies, intense coaches, and parental harassment of officials all communicate to Johnnie that this "kids' game" is somehow very important and very grown up. Is it all for Johnnie or is it for dad and coach?

Consider the perverse interest in winning. It isn't enough to enjoy playing the piano; Suzie has to be the best in town at it. Playing flag football isn't fun if the team doesn't become champions. Playing the game isn't enough; winning is all that counts.

I'm convinced that much of this pressure toward professionalism doesn't originate with the boys and girls; it's applied by parents. Not that anyone loves to lose, either now or when I was a kid.

BUT I BELIEVE ONE THING HAS CHANGED— THE PARENTAL PRESSURE WASN'T THERE IN THE OLD DAYS.

We weren't playing for our folks; we were just playing the game. Never once do I remember any of my friends breaking into tears for striking out in a ball game. We would have thought him bonkers. But I can't count the number of times I've seen today's young players throw their helmets and come from the plate crying. This is a game? (Look, dad, at how much fun we're having!)

To get an idea of how winning at sports is emphasized compared to other things, just try to imagine these same big thirteen and fourteen-year old boys bawling over getting a poor grade in social studies. For me, it's not possible to seriously conjure up such an image.

Though adults shake their heads and claim it's the young people who want to win at all costs, I say it's the adults who have fostered or at least supported that drive, and if they wanted to, the same adults could alter that emphasis.

Another reason children grow up faster today is because of the information they have. Through the marvelous medium of TV, youth today have much more information about the world than did children of previous generations. They also have much more money of their own than ever before, which causes manufacturers and advertisers to target them, and pull them, therefore, more quickly into adulthood.

Perhaps the most startling new aspect of this early pressure to grow up is the growing trend to prepare children for adult success at an early age. Some eight-year-olds confidently state that they are working toward Yale law school entrance. Since, one doesn't get into Yale without being involved through high school in varied activities. So parents start, even before high school, to put their child through ten different activities at a time—sports, music, tutoring, computers— thereby keeping applied the endless pressure for excellence. Where is the time to be a child? Having goals is great, but Yale can wait.

BESIDES THIS SOCIETAL PRESSURE TO GROW UP FAST, THE LDS LIFESTYLE ADDS, IN MANY FAMILIES, ADDITIONAL DIMENSIONS: KEEPING CONSTANTLY BUSY AND BECOMING PERFECT.

Many Latterday Saints seem bent on driving themselves, and their children, to a kind of frenzied rendezvous with the Celestial Kingdom.

Mormons are engaged in lots of things; their reputation as busy, involved people is accurate. Because of our unspoken assumption that "busy is good," some parents use chores, piano lessons, homework, school and church activities—and anything else they can lay hands on—as taskmasters to keep their children busy. They're anxious that no time be "wasted," and they, therefore, fear unstructured time on the part of their children. (At least that's what they say; I think the fact is that some of them are so structured they just don't know there's any other way to live.) While there's some truth in the old saying, "Idle hands are the devil's workshop," like most old sayings, it only tells part of the truth.

Though I happen to have written a book on time-planning for teenagers, I think that concept can be overdone even at that age, and especially at younger ages. The goal isn't to make our youth mini-corporation executives, running from one high-powered activity to another. They'll have time for that later in life if that's their interest.

AT THE RISK OF BEING SIDED WITH THE DEVIL, I WILL STATE MY OPINION THAT PLAIN OLD IDLENESS IS SOMETIMES THE BEST THING AROUND.

I am not worried in the least when I see my children relaxing by doing nothing or by half-heartedly shooting baskets into the shade of the living room floor lamp with a half-deflated balloon. I'll admit to enough Puritanism in me that, if it goes on for *too* long and I suspect there just might be something constructive being postponed, I may ask about homework. If there is none, or if it's finished, then I may suggest reading a book, which is usually enough to send certain of my offspring scurrying to do something—*anything*—else. But what is actually wrong with this kind of leisurely saunter through life on occasion, as long as the important things still get done?

I worry about parents—or rather, I worry about the children of parents—who insist on structuring every minute. The Type-A lifestyle may be very efficient and productive but it has its costs, too.

If we agree that our modern lifestyle needs some monitoring to avoid putting too much pressure on our children, let's look at some ways of reducing those demands to tolerable levels and helping to develop our children into well-adjusted adults.

1. RECONSIDER OBEDIENCE. I've come to believe that one of the most unreasonable demands many of us parents make is for instant, unquestioning obedience at all costs. Is this demand really for the child's good or is it for our own need to feel in control? Such requests for obedience often seem so unnecessary. Of course, obedience as a principle is important, but so are independence and decision-making.

Like most parents when confronted with a challenge to my authority, I have found myself outraged at a child who disobeyed me. And I've sometimes blown the key moment by demanding obedience at all costs, losing sight of what the whole issue was really about.

But isn't obedience good in itself? Well, in my opinion, this is one of those principles that really can't stand alone—it only makes sense when we connect it with something. Obedience to the Nazi party is not something most of us would find a "good" in itself, is it? Out of context, obedience is an abstract that sounds good, but has no meaning.

But, to avoid a semantics argument, if we can agree that what is usually meant by obedience is support of worthwhile activities and requests, then I'll concede that it's a "good." But there are good things and there are better things.

IF WHAT WE'RE REALLY TRYING TO TEACH OUR CHILDREN IS TO TRUST US SO THAT THEY WILL DO THE THINGS WE TELL THEM TO DO, WHY NOT BEGIN TO TEACH THEM TRUST AT AN EARLY AGE, INSTEAD OF CONTINUING TO INSIST ON OBEDIENCE AS AN END IN ITSELF?

Trust seems to me to be a higher virtue than mere obedience. It isn't that obedience is wrong; but a demand for obedience may be a bad way of teaching trust because it gets all hung up with our need for control and our resentfulness if a child challenges us. Then we enter a power struggle in which, even if we "win," we lose, because, in time, the child comes to resent our dominion. We end up with his obedience, but for the wrong reason: fear. And a child may obey out of fear, but he will not trust out of fear. Another way to say it is: he will not trust a dad he fears.

Additionally, overemphasis on any single principle can have bad results. We can continue to demand absolute obedience of our children to the point where they will never learn to think for themselves. In so doing, we will be handicapping them for the future as well as putting needless pressure on them at the present.

2. TEACH REAL VALUES. If you can change the emphasis in your child's thinking from one of competition and accomplishment to one of accepting himself as a worthwhile person who performs for the right reasons, permanent progress will have been made. It's possible to be a member of an intense sports team, for example, and actually enjoy playing! Let the others throw their helmets to the ground when they strike out.

LET YOUR CHILD LEARN TO ENJOY
THE GAME OF LIFE IN ITSELF,
DO HIS BEST, AND SEE THE LOSSES
AS CHALLENGES TO IMPROVE.

Discussions with a child will help you learn what really matters to him. In a case of pressure from peers, it may be that your child finds, when you talk it through with him, that he isn't really interested in some of the things his classmates or teammates find him deficient in. He can then decide that their criticisms don't matter and the pressure is reduced. It's the talking about it with you that's the key to helping him see what's important.

3. NEVER SHAME. Have you ever used the ultimate in the repertoire of subtle emotional abuses, "I'm ashamed of you"? This is perhaps the worst thing a child can hear from his dad. It's one thing to find that a parent is upset with our actions, but to have him feel ashamed of us is to feel removed from the circle of love and outside the accepted family group. How does one get back in?

Pressure like this is very harmful to the child because he sees no way of changing your mind. He can't force you to not be ashamed. And, to him, being ashamed means you don't want to be around him, don't like him, and maybe don't even love him. It comes across as conditional love at its worst.

4. REDUCE PRESSURE TO CONFORM. A pressure that can be reduced by a parent is the stereotyping that tells a child he can't be himself. This is done in the way some parents push their family heritage down their child's throat.

"We don't do that in *our* family," can be a useful tool to induce pride in better behavior, or it can be a lever to exert excessive control. If overused, the reaction is likely to be that the child says, "Then I guess I'm not a member of this family," and rejects the demands of a heritage he's now learned not to value anyway.

IF IT MEANS REJECTING SOME VAGUE
HERITAGE OR BECOMING HIS OWN

PERSON, NEARLY EVERY CHILD WILL, IN TIME, REJECT THE HERITAGE.

It's a choice no one should be forced to make.

Feeling part of a group, a heritage, or a family tradition, is a great thing, but it can only go so far. Heritage provides a framework to build on in developing individual personalities. But if that structure becomes an end in itself, tradition can become a jail. And, sooner or later—at fifteen, at twenty-five, at forty-five—personalities break out of jail or they bottle up a great deal of resentment that they were never allowed to be anything other than part of the framework, rather than an individual.

Be a gentle teacher, one who shows the way, rather than forces into conformity. Remember, dad, all lessons can't be learned at once. Look for key moments. Continue to work with and help your children, but keep in mind that helping is a long way from nagging and carping.

Just because America is a great place and the LDS lifestyle offers a great deal in the way of positive values doesn't mean that good things don't have their negative by-products. Be aware of how the pressures you've adjusted to as adults, perhaps over several years, might affect your child, who hasn't yet had time to adjust, and who spends so much effort subconsciously and consciously trying to please you.

Your child will assume that you accept all the cultural mores around you, such as winning at all costs and growing up fast, unless you tone them down some in importance. Make your home a place where unnecessary demands are reduced, making way for a more healthy way of looking at life.

Topics For Discussion With Your Wife

1. How much pressure do we add to our children's lives? How much of this is needless?

2. Do we accept our children as they are? Do they know this? How do they know it? What are some instances that might tell them otherwise, and how can these be changed?

3. How do we feel about the "instant adulthood" America supplies today? Is it harmful? In what ways? Is it beneficial? In what ways?

4. How do we feel about unstructured time for our children? Are we always trying to keep them busy? Are they busy enough, too busy, or do they need more to do?

5. How much obedience do we demand? At what age in our children do we expect thinking for themselves and a reduction in orders from us? Do we agree on the level of obedience desired?

6. Are there values we would like to teach our children that haven't been adequately taught yet? What are our plans for teaching those?

7. Do we use shame as a motivator?

8. Do we demand conformity because of family name or heritage? How much autonomy are we able to allow our children?

9. How much in agreement are we on the ideas in this chapter? Are we working together? Have we identified areas of difference, and are we able to talk about them? Are there major areas we need to discuss further at a future time?

9

Allow and Cause Growth

Let's talk about human potential.

Abandoned in the hospital at birth, baby Leslie was taken home by a nurse to give him a place to die. Doctors said his multiple mental and physical defects promised him but a few weeks of survival. They were wrong; in the hands of nurse May Lemke, Leslie lived. However, he was severely retarded, blind, and totally unresponsive to sound or touch.

May carried and cared for him, hoping he might eventually learn and be able to communicate, but for years and years, no progress was seen. One day a great thing occurred: by holding on to a chain-link fence in the Lemke's back yard, Leslie stood alone for the first time in his life. He was sixteen years old.

Encouraged, May felt there must be a way to reach into the heart of this young man and get a response, but constant talking to him elicited nothing. Now nearly twenty years old, Leslie had never spoken a word. At about this time May and her husband decided to play the radio or phonograph all day every day in their home—hoping that music might somehow reach Leslie. But he showed no interest. The Lemke's bought a piano and placed Leslie's fingers on the keys. No response. But the recorded music still played on in the Lemke home.

Then one night something happened that can only be called a miracle. May awoke at 3 a.m. to hear piano music. Supposing the phonograph had somehow been left playing, she went to the living room.

There she saw something she never could have imagined. At the piano, playing Tschaikovsky's Piano Concerto No. 1, sat Leslie. Leslie, who had never before got out of bed on his own, never seated himself at the piano, never even struck a key, now played a difficult classical composition with grace and expression. It was unbelievable.

From that memorable moment on, Leslie could play everything he had passively listened to over the years—classical and pop, country-western and soul, advertising jingles—all by ear.

Over the years since then, Leslie and May have appeared on the *Phil Donahue Show*, Public Television has done a special on their story, and it was reported in the October 1982 *Reader's Digest*. Incidentally, May was right; music was a turning point for Leslie, whose soul was somehow finally unstopped. He began to communicate vocally, first with single words, and eventually with complete sentences.

How can it be explained? How does one who was never able to "learn" anything, one who can't begin to learn to read music and who doesn't even know the names or locations of the notes, sit down and play difficult classical works by ear? What incalculable capacity is inherent in the human mind? What capacity was there in this truly "uneducable" brain, seemingly uninterested and unattending to the outside world, that could enable Leslie to reproduce complex music heard months before? What "normal" person could match such a miracle? And what does this tell us about the potential in all of us, including our own children?

Similar reports have appeared about other "slow learners" who know no math rules but who arrive, in their heads, at instant answers to complex math questions.

"What is 3762 multiplied by 8695?"

The answer, "32,710,590," comes from a child with an IQ of 37, a child who cannot learn the simplest standard rules of multiplication. And the answer comes instantly, before a math professor can punch in the numbers on a calculator!

Another "uneducable" paints high-priced masterpieces of vividly-detailed scenes he has merely glimpsed years before. "Normal" people can't recall such detail.

Something is happening in these minds that we don't begin to have an explanation for.

WHAT INCREDIBLE STRENGTH THERE MUST BE IN EACH OF US IF WE COULD LEARN HOW TO UNLEASH IT.

And yet, dads, we sometimes berate our children for being "dumb" or "slow" because they may not have caught on to some task quite as quickly as we think they should. On such occasions we would do well to remember May Lemke, who waited sixteen years for Leslie's first step and nearly twenty for his first word. Most of us would have given up long before that. We would have certainly decided that Leslie could never achieve, wouldn't we?

But human potential is enormous; and it's there in all of us, even in those sometimes exasperating children of ours. The challenge is to provide an attitude and an atmosphere that will allow this potential to be unleashed. And a dad can be a powerful agent in bringing out this God-given potential in his children.

Allowing our children to develop their own potential is an idea we all agree with in concept, but it turns out to be one of the hardest things most of us do. It requires us to step back a little because our children can only learn to run their own lives when we let them. And we don't like to let go.

What do we want for our children? In the short run, I believe all parents want the same things. We'd like our kids to be happy, at peace, successful in the important things in life, to feel good about themselves, to have an enjoyable—even carefree—childhood.

Although most parents want happiness for their children, not all parents have thought about how to prepare them to earn this happiness themselves.

THE BEST LONG-TERM PARENTAL GOAL WOULD NOT BE TO GIVE OUR CHILDREN HAPPINESS, BUT TO TEACH THEM HOW TO ACHIEVE IT.

Rather than asking what we want for our *children*, we might better ask, "What do we want for the *adults* our children are going to be for most of their lives?" We're not just raising kids; we're raising people. They will very soon be on their own, away from our direct influence. The happiness, peace, and success we tried to provide them in their youth can only carry over to their adulthood if they have learned to create these qualities on their own. Unfortunately, these attributes can't be passed down to someone else like the family china can, but have to be created anew by each generation.

But it's clear that the perfect child doesn't always become the perfect adult. Some of those so solicitously fussed over as children end up not finding much happiness as adults. Not only do they sometimes not have the skills necessary to achieve happiness, but they may not even know there *are* such skills, or that happiness requires effort. They just keep waiting for happiness to "happen" to them, like drawing a winning lottery ticket.

Then just what is the perfect adult? Well, one characteristic we would expect to find in the fully functioning, capable adult is a rational, intelligent decision-making ability. Now, any dad would say he wants his children to grow into thinking, independent agents able to make their own way in the world. Then his eighteen-year-old puts too much sugar on his cornflakes or commits some other mortal sin, and dad jumps all over him. Stating our belief in independence isn't the same as having carefully considered our actions and attitudes to see if they are actually in line with our assertions.

Here is a hard question, dad: Do we want our children to grow up or not? Of course, we say. But, on the other hand, maybe not really. Little kids are easier to enjoy, keep happy, and have fun with, not to mention boss around, put to bed, and farm out to baby-sitters. As young parents, we're full of child-rearing ideas to try out, we're *needed* in our children's lives—and it's nice to be needed—and, best of all, we're in control. So we sometimes continue "taking care" of our children to the point of interference.

MUCH OF WHAT "STANDARD" PARENTING DOES IS COUNTER-PRODUCTIVE TO LETTING CHILDREN DEVELOP THEIR OWN DECISION-MAKING ABILITIES.

What are some of the areas where parents could better allow their kids to grow into responsible adults?

1. DECISION-MAKING PRACTICE. Kids aren't going to learn to think for themselves without being given the chance. There is no other way for young people to learn that their choices have consequences, be they good, bad, or mixed, than to be allowed to make their own decisions and required to accept the consequences. We all learn best from our own experience.

But our children's choices might be poor ones and might even hurt them, we fear. So we interfere and make decisions for them. If we parents are always there to protect our kids from failure by stepping in to "save" them when they make poor choices, they're not learning what they need to learn. If we underwrite their decisions so they can't fail, we actually prevent our kids from learning from their choices.

Parents hate for their kids to fail. But perhaps we ought to ask: just how harmful is failure, really? What if our children don't succeed in all things? In the long run, might not a relatively small failure now teach insights that could prevent bigger failures later on? Rushing in to save our children too often might even set them up for *certain* failure later.

Certainly there are times when intervention on a child's behalf might be necessary. But I find many parents much too eager to prevent any negative effects—the natural consequences of poor decisions—from coming to their children, even when the effects are minor and relatively harmless.

Paraphrasing what has been said about despots, the problem with the parent who constantly interferes to save his child is not that he doesn't love his children enough; it's that he loves them too much—and trusts them too little—to let them make appropriate decisions for themselves.

One example of trusting kids to make important decisions early in life occurs in the Glade family, where the names of all the children are on the family checkbook. As soon as each child is old enough to understand how checks work, he or she can write a check anytime. The system works. The children learn to manage money and to be sure they really need something before spending family money on it.

Think of the sense of trust these children know their parents have in them. All the lectures in the world about wise money use couldn't replace the learning provided by such an act of trust on the part of the parents in the Glade household.

Unlike the Glades, most of us *talk* about teaching our children responsibility but are afraid to try it in significant ways. Our children might fail. They might burn the roast, spend too much, inconvenience us. Or, worst of all, they might embarrass us in the eyes of our neighbors or friends.

IF WE ARE COMMITTED TO INDEPENDENCE IN OUR CHILDREN, JUST AS WE VALUE IT IN OURSELVES, WE WILL NEED TO PROVIDE OPPORTUNITIES FOR THEM TO MAKE MANY OF THEIR OWN DECISIONS.

A child who goes out into the world to college or into marriage, and who has been not been given the chance to make oodles and scads of decisions before getting to that point, is bound to have troubles. Some young people "go wild" when out on their own for the first time—intoxicated by the choices available to them—because they have never had any real freedom up to that point. They don't have any more idea where to start than does a mouse who wanders into a cheese factory. Some parents discover to their sorrow that the protection they tried to give their child has turned to his detriment when he's faced with real decisions and no practice in making them.

Decision-making isn't an idea or a concept that can be learned just by *talking* about it; it's a skill—and, therefore, requires *practice*. If you knew your child at eighteen or twenty would be thrown into the ocean, would you give him swimming practice from his earliest years, or would you keep him away from the pool?

Eventually, your child will be thrown into a sea of decision-making. You can help your child make decisions while under your care—in the backyard swimming pool, as it were—where he can be rescued if necessary, or you can wait and let him flounder later, far out to sea.

"Ah," you say, "but if I follow these ideas, I will end up with a child who doesn't need my store of wisdom. And there's nothing worse than a seventeen-year old 'know-it-all' who won't take dad's advice."

Oh, yes, there is. It's a thirty-five-year-old who can't decide whether to rearrange the furniture without calling home. Insolence is always better than wimpiness. The passing years have ways of beating down the arrogant to more tolerable levels. But those with stunted self-esteems face a lifelong, tremendously difficult battle.

Of course, creating arrogant brats isn't really the goal either. If you've established the proper relationship, that seventeen-year-old—although sure he already has the answers —will occasionally ask your advice, if for no other reason than to see if the old man still remembers the questions.

2. FACING LIFE. When I was very young, my folks lived on a large ranch where dad milked a dairy herd and kept a few horses. One day dad gave me a colt of my own. I was very excited about this colt, as only a five- or six-year-old can be. Whether I actually remember what he looked like or whether my memory has been enhanced by the old black and white photograph I have of him, I don't honestly know. But there's one indelible memory that doesn't come from a picture. It's my remembrance of the day my colt died.

He'd been out to pasture with the other horses, but hadn't been seen for several days. My dad rode out to look for him. Maybe I even rode with him, I'm not sure. But at least in my mind I can see my colt lying dead on the ground.

We all have memories of our first encounters with such serious matters as birth and death; my colt experience isn't unique. Though my own children have never lived on a ranch, we've buried two cats, four gerbils, and two zebra finches in the last few years.

All of these have been serious moments. It pains a dad to see his children cry over lost pets. We might have it otherwise, if we could, to protect our children. But we also know they have to learn to face such things. Since we cannot change the way the world works, part of our job, as parents, is to teach our children that life includes death, failure, sorrow, mistakes, and troubles. As the sun shines today, tomorrow there may be clouds. To fail to prepare a child to cope with this possibility is to deprive him of necessary opportunities to adjust and grow.

One summer day, a few years ago, Alysa, then perhaps three or four years old, was walking barefoot on the lawn when she suddenly yelped. A bee had stung her on the foot. When she stopped yelling enough to talk, she made a statement illustrating the strong concept of fairness that children carry. "It stung me," she wept, "And I didn't do anything to *it*."

Ah, there's the rub. Things hurt us when we don't deserve it. Diseases strike kind and compassionate people. Earthquakes shatter nurseries and schools.

I'm not trying to elicit tears. I'm just reminding us that life is not fair. We all know it isn't, but, deep down, none of us wants to believe it isn't. When it's *our* family that has been struck, we still ask "Why me?" as if our pondering of some master balance scale might help us find the "fairness" in the event. But there is no apparent fairness. And since none of us likes the idea that there isn't, we often want to shelter our children from the harsh elements of life.

IT'S A NATURAL ENOUGH PARENTAL DESIRE TO WANT TO SHELTER OUR OFFSPRING. BUT IT CAN'T BE DONE.

The most we can do is delay the hurt, and sometimes that isn't the best thing to do. In extreme cases, parents who have lost a child have tried to avoid speaking of him or her, to protect their other young children from supposed pain. But these children need a chance to mourn too.

In other households, the death of a grandparent is treated as nothing but a blessed event. "Grandpa is now free of pain," we tell our children cheerily, "and has gone to live with Heavenly Father," as if he's just taking a little airplane trip someplace for Christmas. It may take little Suzie's, "But we still miss him, don't we?" to help us realize that, religious faith and practical acceptance aside, death still leaves a real void no one else can fill—one that will never again be filled. And that's a sad fact, so why pretend it isn't?

The pretense that all is well under such circumstances is unnatural, confusing, and inhibiting of true emotional expression in a child. Such events need to be discussed, felt, and wept over by all concerned, including the young ones.

Why not treat the death of a loved one as a key moment you can use to teach your child a great deal about life? It calls for grief on the part of the children as well as the adults; they needn't be sheltered from it. Let it come; grief is natural and it is cleansing.

Life will not always go the way our children hope it will. Our task is to prepare them so that they can look back later and see the benefit in difficult times. As someone said, "If it doesn't kill you outright, it will make you better."

WE MUST TRY TO PREPARE OUR CHILDREN TO ACCEPT DIFFICULTIES AS PART OF LIFE AND TO GROW FROM THEM.

I'm not advocating a pessimistic, morbid inculcating of our youth with the woes of the world. For a third grader to fret about possible nuclear destruction is neither healthy nor necessary. But neither is it realistic or wise to unduly protect young people from feeling a full range of emotions.

Teaching youth to face difficulties can mean appearing cruel and heartless in refusing to do for them what they can and should do for themselves. When the Zirker's twelve-year-old son, David, broke his arm, he found the cast more than a little inhibiting for one of his two-handed chores—milking the cow. However, his negotiations with his dad to take over the job got him nowhere. "I'm supposed to milk a cow with one hand?" he asked. It sounded impossible. But dad was firm. Why? Because he, himself, had done that same chore under the same conditions when he was young.

At first, both the cow and the family suffered. But, soon, the bucket was as full as ever. When David discovered that a cow could be milked with one hand, he also found that he could write his term paper as well as attend Scout camp, both of which he had assumed he couldn't do without the use of both hands. (Ron and Sherri Zirker, "Teaching Teens Self-Discipline," *The Ensign*, April 1982)

What a valuable lesson this young man learned about his abilities when no one pampered him. But how hard it is for us, as parents, to teach such lessons without giving in to our guilt, or our fear of being thought of as "mean" parents. If we could only learn to live with the label of "demanding" parents who expect a lot from their children—but no more than they are capable of giving—we would know that meanness has nothing to do with it.

Being a good parent means being a strong parent. Kindness is a great trait, but if kindness robs our kids of learning other traits—like self-reliance—then it isn't kindness, it's weakness. Sometimes being a good dad demands a degree of loving toughness.

3. ACCEPTING THE DECISIONS YOUR KIDS MAKE. How good are you at letting your children be themselves, at letting them be at the level they are? Do you demand that they move right now to the level where you want them to be and make the choices you would make? Do you want them to see everything your way? Your parental inclination is to want your kids to grow and improve, and your duty is to show them what you consider the better way. But what if they don't agree? What if they're listening to Thoreau's "different drummer"?

Are you willing to allow your son not to get his Eagle Scout award if he chooses not to? Would you pressure, coerce, demand, and push him to do so, "for his own good," especially, I might ask, if it's something *you* value and have looked forward to his receiving? Or if you regret not having attained it yourself? Or if you did attain it and feel you've started a family tradition?

IS YOUR EGO SECURE ENOUGH THAT YOUR CHILDREN CAN TAKE A PATH DIFFERENT FROM THE ONE YOU WOULD HAVE CHOSEN FOR THEM?

Every dad must face the uncomfortable question: How much of your effort to "help" your children is to help yourself, feed your ego, build your image, or cover your own fears?

A related question is whether a child must magnify a talent he's uninterested in just because he's good at the thing. Some parents talk as if a child *must* perform on the violin because "he has such an obvious talent." Does he have no choice, therefore?

To expose youth to opportunities to use their talents, and to encourage them to spend time in positive ways is part of your job as a dad. There's no harm in reminders, urgings, perhaps even a little coercion to practice the violin. You may wish to reward a child by doing a chore for him if he'll spend that time practicing. But beware of attitudes that leave your child no choice. If he'd rather do dishes than play the piano, accept that—for now at least—the piano holds little charm.

If someone tested you, dad, and found a remarkable native ability with the bagpipes, I'll bet that—after the honor wore off—you would demand some say in whether that meant you *had* to practice it and tote it in your best kilt in the next parade. If *you* don't feel compelled to do something just because you have the ability, give your sons and daughters the same latitude.

Rebellion can be the norm for teenagers who haven't been allowed to make choices. "You're good at it; you'll do it," leaves them wondering if they really have any options or if the minute their choices disagree with yours, their freedom is removed. Perhaps if they felt they had the right to make real choices in these lesser matters, they wouldn't feel the need to exert their independence in the greater matters.

SINCE THE SEARCH FOR INDEPENDENCE OFTEN BRINGS OUT REBELLION IN SOME FORM IN ADOLESCENTS, WHY NOT LET THEM "REBEL" IN SOMETHING SAFE?

If refusing to play the Paraguayan harp lets them get rebellion out of their system, let them refuse. If their insurrection is as innocuous as purple hair and strange clothing styles, or dropping out of music lessons, be glad it's nothing more.

4. SUPPORT OF PAST CHOICES. Once you let your children make decisions, how willing are you to support them? You would have chosen differently but the choice wasn't yours. You expressed your views; they weren't accepted. It's settled. Now what do you do? Support or undermine?

One mother was naturally upset when her daughter went to live with a man rather than marrying him. Since this went against everything the parents had taught their child, their concern was great. The mother often spoke with her daughter about putting things right by getting married. At the time, the daughter didn't see the need. Years went by.

Finally, on her own, the daughter decided to marry the man. But since the decision wasn't done at her timing, the mother did not rejoice and support the decision. She was sure the daughter had an ulterior motive, that she was planning to move out on the man— and wanted to say that she had married and divorced him rather than just having lived with him.

The mother just had to be right. She wouldn't let her daughter change except on the mother's terms. She had failed her daughter at a key moment by not rejoicing at the announcement of the marriage.

I'm not concerned here with the rightness or wrongness of the daughter's actions; I'm just pointing out that, once a decision is out of our hands as a parent, once we've done our best to teach correct principles, our role now is to be supportive and to not weaken the relationship.

THERE COMES A TIME FOR SUPPORT, AFTER WE HAVE MADE OUR VIEWS CLEAR.

People who disown their children miss this point entirely. Children can't disown us for some of our outrageous actions; the reverse shouldn't happen either. Some parents feel so strongly the need to always stand for what they feel is right that they can't give support when a child chooses other than what the parents would have chosen. The relationship is therefore needlessly harmed.

A dad should have views and he should express them, but, once a decision is out of his hands, rejecting the child for making the decision is an artificial, self-serving stance. Dad can mourn over it if necessary, but then he must get on with living and loving his child.

If you can show your support and understanding for their honest decisions, you will have taken a big step toward helping your children create growth instead of failure. Although it might not be easy, a regular dad can do it.

If we give our children opportunities for growth, we would expect that one day they would take total control of their own lives. At what age will your children arrive at this point, so terrifying to parents, of running their own lives? At twenty-one? Twenty-five? After graduate school? Nope, too late.

J.D. Sanderson proposes an answer that sounds revolutionary in modern America. In most states the *law* recognizes the concept, but many *parents* don't seem to. It's this:

IT'S POSSIBLE TO RAISE CHILDREN WHO ARE ADULT AT 18, READY TO TAKE ON THE WORLD AND MAKE THEIR OWN DECISIONS.

Let's look at Sanderson's idea. American middle-class youngsters are coddled, he says. Many American parents have come to feel that they owe more than is reasonable to their children.

Although we think we're doing them a favor, what we're really teaching kids when we provide their every request is to depend on mom and dad to pull them along. What they miss out on are discipline, hard work, and self-denial—the very traits that could guide them through life's inevitable tough times. (Very likely these are the traits that put the parents in the position of being capable of offering the help!)

Here's a summary of Sanderson's "Adult-at-Eighteen" plan. It's a five-year program starting on your child's thirteenth birthday. After singing "Happy Birthday," tell her that you have some new rules that she's going to love. Now that she's a teenager, there are some things she can handle entirely on her own. You will no longer concern yourself with the condition of her room, her grooming or dress, her sleeping hours, or her nutrition. She may live in a clean or a messy room, go to bed as late as she chooses, and wear and eat what she wishes.

All of this will be a thrill to the child, who will feel it's about time. Though she isn't quite as grown up as she thinks, none of these four freedoms is likely to hurt her, even if she doesn't handle each of them as you would prefer. And she is going to learn a great deal about running her own life as she gains decision-making experience.

Later, other agreements are made about having the child assume greater household responsibilities, find her own transportation, when possible, and earn part of her own support. (See Jim Sanderson, *How to Raise Your Kids to Stand on Their Own Two Feet*, New York, Congdon & Weed, Inc., 1978)

These are the rules that you and your child will live with for the next few years. These need not be extreme or overly rigid. There will be times when you will drive your child to where she needs to go. It's her attitude of expecting it that you're trying to change. She probably can't earn enough money for all of her own clothing. But she can contribute and, in the process, learn that she is becoming more and more capable of taking care of herself. Her room may be a disaster, she may stay up too late, wear clothes you find more than strange, and eat Twinkies for breakfast—bought with her own money, of course—but these are all relatively harmless "practice runs" at decision-making.

SINCE SOME OF YOUR CHILD'S CHOICES AREN'T YOUR PREFERENCES, DAD, HERE'S THE HARD PART: KEEP YOUR MOUTH SHUT, JUST AS YOU SAID YOU WOULD.

These choices aren't going to hurt your child any more than they would hurt the kid down the street, and you don't spend time worrying about what *she* eats for breakfast, do you? How harmful can these small matters be compared to the independence your child is gaining? (And think of what *you* are learning about tolerance and patience, although at first your tongue may develop a deep groove in it, from having to bite it so often.)

Hardhearted? By some standards, yes. For the good of your offspring? Absolutely. Either they're adult at eighteen or they're not. Either you're serious about this idea or you're not. You may select an age other than eighteen; the principle still holds: you and your child are working toward a goal that you both support—eventual, responsible independence, with a graduation date specified.

You'll always be a parent. You won't step out of your child's life entirely at eighteen, nor necessarily kick her out of the house, but the expectations under such a system are now vastly different from before. A great deal of learning will occur in a relatively safe setting. The types of choices your child will make under the five-year preparation time will be made *somewhere, sometime* anyway. Why not in the controlled atmosphere of your home, under your silent surveillance?

We won't always agree with the choices our children make. Occasionally as a parent we may even have to intervene to "save" them, but as they get older, these occurrences should be rare. We can counsel with them, guide them, and help them, but we must remember that each individual is responsible for his own life and his only.

A parent can "keep a child in his place," or "let him find his place." Both approaches come from parents who love their children. But which view shows more long-term perspective and trust? Which one results, in the long run, in more real love? Growth can only occur in an atmosphere of trust where real experience is given, with the possibilities of mistakes, improvement, and growth—a never-ending cycle that will continue throughout life.

It isn't easy unselfishly to allow our children to grow in their own ways. Carole Barnes tells of her middle son, David, who is different from other boys in mental capacity. He knows he is not the same as his older and his younger brothers and calls himself, "the middlest boy of all."

Carole's desires for him to be like other boys leads her into a difficult struggle with herself which finally results in her realization that forcing him into the mold of others will only cause him unhappiness, since he truly does "hear a different drummer." She knows she must let him be what he can be, and realizes that he is happiest in a special-care village of people of similar capacity. Her acceptance is complete when she learns that he is doing well there, at his own level.

She writes: "We are proud, my husband and I, of all our sons. The biggest boy of our house is a fine athlete, the leading track man in his school. The littlest boy is a good student, standing at the top of his class. And the middlest boy of our house—David—is the very best laundry worker in the village where he lives." (Carole Barnes, "The Middlest Boy of All," *Reader's Digest*, April 1968)

Topics For Discussion With Your Wife

1. How willing are we to allow our children to set their own course in life? How much do we force them into our patterns? Are we guides or drill sergeants?

2. How much do we let our children make their own decisions? Do we look for ways to give them practice at it? How tolerant are we of errors, mistakes and immature solutions? How likely are we to step in to "save" our children from their poor decisions?

3. How successfully have we prepared our children to accept the fact that life will be hard, but that people can learn from disappointments? How much do we protect them life's realities?

4. How much latitude do we allow our children in making their own choices about using their talents? Where does encouragement leave off and coercion begin?

5. How willing are we to give support to our children after they've made a decision? Do we continue to let them know that they've made a mistake and that we're going to harangue them until they fix the situation to our liking? Do we look to the past or to the future?

6. How effectively have we been able to "let go" as our children mature? Do we treat them differently as they get older and more capable?

7. How committed are we to the idea of "adult at eighteen"? Do both of us agree on it? Do our children know about the plan? Are we consistent in working toward that goal?

8. How much in agreement are we on the ideas in this chapter? Are we working together? Have we identified areas of difference, and are we able to talk about them? Are there major areas we need to discuss further at a future time?

10

Teach How to Live

Teaching values for successful living is one of a dad's greatest responsibilities. And whether or not we choose to do so *deliberately*, we all teach values all the time. We don't sit down and teach them as arithmetic is taught, but values are being taught in our homes right now.

In our culture, we talk of honesty, diligence, and frugality, to name three traditional American values. Nearly every American parent would say he wants his offspring to live by these values. But others are considerably less conspicuous. For example, at this moment, by your free-will reading of this book, rather than spending your time trimming your toenails, you are expressing a value about books and reading. And if you read books often in the presence of your family, though it may never occur to you to preach them a sermon on the virtues of reading, you are "teaching" a value.

THE MAIN POINT ABOUT TEACHING VALUES IS THAT WE TEACH WHAT WE ARE.

We all teach who we are all the time, like it or not, generally when we're giving the least thought to it. Let's give thought to it, to see if we can do better at passing on to our children those things we find valuable.

There's a reason to make this a conscious consideration. While we're always teaching who we are, certain individual values don't

116

get communicated very well without a special effort to teach them, because they aren't visible.

To carry one step further the example of reading this book, consider that it's possible for a dad who does value reading to do all of his reading in bed after his children are asleep. Therefore, they never see him reading. He may someday be surprised to find that his children don't read. In this case his reading value was invisible to his family members because they just never saw him do it.

Parents are sometimes surprised to realize that some of their most basic values are invisible.

"How could my kid shoplift?" they agonize. "We've always been honest."

And so they have. But on how many occasions did their children see them "being honest"? Were the children always there when mom returned the extra change to the clerk, or when dad told the prospective buyer the defects in the old car he was selling, or when they filled out their income tax returns honestly? Such object lessons need to be discussed to make the point. Otherwise, young people may not notice them at all.

In this sense, the old aphorism about teaching by "example, example, example," hasn't ever seemed quite sufficient to me. Often added discussion and clarification are needed to make the example visible. "Setting a good example" of the value of work by working hard yourself, for example, hoping it will rub off on your children, will succeed about as well as trying to teach a pig to pirouette by taking her to the ballet each week. Only discussion of the value of work and real sweat—their own—will teach kids to work. And so it is with many things we try to teach.

An interesting study showed that nearly half the American parents studied claimed they wanted their children to learn the "traditional" values of their grandparents' day: saving money, working hard, putting duty before pleasure, and "my country, right or wrong." Yet most of those people, when questioned about their own lives, don't live those values themselves, at least not to the degree their grandparents did. There is a discrepancy between code words that sound good and actual lives of the survey respondents. It wouldn't be hard to guess whether it was the words or the lives that taught their offspring the most, would it? And that's one difficulty in teaching values.

OFTEN WE TRY TO TEACH ABSTRACTS WE HAVEN'T APPLIED OURSELVES. WHAT WE SAY DOESN'T MATCH WHAT WE DO.

If we recognized the discrepancies, we could admit them, point out our shortcomings, and urge our children to do better. But, as a society, we don't often recognize the discrepancies. We think we value saving money, but our credit card accounts show otherwise. We claim to work hard, but we boast about what we get away with on the job. We say we put our country first, but we find ways to cheat on our taxes. Words against deeds. In that battle, words lose every time.

So far, I've tried to make two points:

First, that a little self-scrutiny will help us know what we're really teaching when our words don't match our deeds. Second, that some values are rather invisible and require more than just example to pass them on to the next generation.

Let's look at ways to improve our results in passing on values that we esteem.

1. OFFER REINFORCEMENT. If we expect to teach values without reinforcement, we won't get far. Complimenting our children when they even *lean* a little bit toward the value we espouse will go a long ways toward fixing it in their minds. Don't assume that a child knows he is a good peacemaker, for example. He may not have any comparisons. He needs you to tell him that you've looked around the household, the neighborhood, and the county, and that, in your transcendent judgment, he's the best peacemaker in sight.

2. TRY ROLE-PLAYING. Values can't be learned in a vacuum. Though we may teach honesty, kindness, or diligence, there will be no true learning until our children encounter these concepts in real situations or in simulated situations such as role-playing.

In role-playing, there are no "right" answers and only honest responses are of any value. Otherwise the dialogue soon degenerates into what the children think a parent wants to hear. Casualness and allowing children to skip a portion without feeling pressured are also necessary.

Role-playing is a great way to get children to think through what they value as they encounter situations similar to what real life offers them. The costume kit and makeup aren't necessary to put our children into a setting realistic enough to see how they would respond. "What if. . .?" questions at the dinner table or any other casual setting are adequate.

Consider the following dinner-table dialogue to see how this idea works. (Don't worry about following a script. The conversation will lead where it will.)

DAD: "Janie, I'll bet there are people with drugs at your junior high."

JANIE: "Oh, yes, anybody can get drugs there."

DAD: "Has anyone ever approached you to use them?"

JANIE: "No, but I've known people who had them."

DAD: "What if someone did approach you? Let's say you're at your locker between classes, nobody is around, and a friend or someone you look up to comes up and says, 'Hey, Janie, I've got two joints here. Want to try one?' What would you say?"

JANIE, laughing: "Oh, I don't know, dad. I'd just say no."

(At this point, Janie may need help to get serious about how to handle this incident if it really happened. Maybe the subject is too close to home. Or her laugh may indicate that she's nervous about considering it at the dinner table. If so, dad might just drop the subject for now and pick it up in a different setting. Later, dad goes to Janie's room to continue the dialogue.)

DAD: "Janie, at dinner, you gave the right answer in saying no to drugs. But I wasn't sure we really considered how hard that answer might be to give in a real situation. Could we continue for a minute from where we left off?"

JANIE: "OK, dad."

DAD: "We were to the point where someone asked if you wanted a marijuana smoke. Could this happen?"

JANIE: "Oh, yes, it could happen."

DAD: "Suppose this is a girl older than you—an eighth-grader—whom you have looked up to, maybe a class or school officer, someone you didn't suspect would use drugs. You've wanted to be her friend, but you haven't had much occasion to be around her. Now, she offers you drugs. What do you do?"

JANIE: "I'd still say no."

DAD: "Janie, I don't want to push this too far. I believe you would say no, and I'm proud of you for that. But I want to make the point that it's hard to say no sometimes. If a scummy old man in dark glasses called to you from a dark alley and offered you something, it would be pretty simple to say 'no' compared to saying it to a person you admire. Do you see what I mean?

"Coming from someone you admire, the invitation might make you sort of wonder whether drugs could be all that bad. After all, this neat person uses them. That's why I'm describing the situation in this much detail and trying to get you to really put yourself in that position.

"So, if you just say no to this girl, you take a chance that she will never be your friend, and that could be very important to you. I think a lot of kids would hedge a little at that point, and maybe say something more like, 'Well, not this time, thanks,' you know, to keep her friendship. Just plain 'no' is kind of abrupt, isn't it?"

JANIE: "I see what you mean, dad. And I think it would be hard to say no to her, if I wanted her for a friend. But I've thought about this before, and I would still say no. I think what I would actually say is: 'No. I don't use that stuff.' Then if I was really brave, I might even say, 'I didn't know you did, either. Why do you?' "

This dialogue could go on with dad playing the role of the other girl. If the dialogue strengthens Janie in a situation she may not have thought through before, then it's better than a sermon any day. Janie obviously doesn't *plan* to use drugs. What role-playing may do is to help her plan *not* to use drugs. There's a difference.

The session could end with a compliment to Janie on her honesty, and dad's reassurance that he wasn't doubting her, that he was just trying to help her see what the pressures are that can make resisting hard for even the most dedicated people.

Role-playing shouldn't be turned into a preaching session. If the answers trouble us, we know what to work on with that child. The goal is to get the child to think about how she would feel to be in these situations, not just to give the answers she knows a parent wants to hear.

3. JUST TALK. Casual conversation between you and your children is one of the main ways they learn about the world. Many of

us may spend more time shopping for our children and planning outings and activities for them than we do in just talking. Conversation mustn't be underrated as a way to teach. I still remember comments my parents made, long ago, about political figures and issues of that day.

Perhaps the advice in this section that will seem the strangest is this: children can benefit from talking about people. No, I'm not advocating gossip, backbiting, or bitter comparisons of neighbors one to another. But I believe that analyzing people, noticing them and discussing what they do, can be very instructive and need not be accusatory nor attacking.

WE'VE ALWAYS BEEN TAUGHT NOT TO TALK ABOUT PEOPLE BECAUSE IT WOULD SOUND NEGATIVE AND JUDGMENTAL. BUT IF HANDLED PROPERLY, SUCH TALK CAN TEACH GREATER ACCEPTANCE OF OTHERS.

The extreme we've been told to avoid is condemning actions we don't like because this can teach rejection—not only of their actions, but of the people involved. Out of fear of sounding judgmental, then, people might follow the maxim, "If you can't say something nice about people, don't say anything at all," to the point where they can't open their mouths. Any mention of others strikes them as negative. But to discuss what people do and why we suppose they do it isn't necessarily not being "nice."

Why can't actions that differ from ours be brought up in a way that illustrates that other people have a viewpoint, too, and have a right to it? While they're young, children have the best chance to learn acceptance of those with different views. If they can understand that almost everyone has a viewpoint that makes some sense from their perspective, they will fear the world less and be more willing to look for ways to accommodate and solve, rather than fight and complicate.

4. DISCUSS TELEVISION. TV is one of the most effective teachers there is. Of course it doesn't always teach what we want our children to learn, but it can be used to help teach positive values if dis-

cussion is added to the viewing. In spite of monitoring, our children will see and hear things on TV that are not always in tune with our parental values. To take the ax to the picture tube is, to me, an over-reaction. How much better to discuss the objectionable, strange, or distorted material that comes over the air.

Not only can a dad make it clear that the car chase scenes are dangerously misleading, and that he had better not ever hear of any of his kids driving in this cartoon-like style, but other points can be made from some of the odd lifestyles shown. Point out that good drama doesn't often make good living.

Have you noticed that, in TV and movies, almost never is a dialogue shown where two characters sit down and talk out a resolution? People portrayed on TV rarely listen to each other. Typically, they stand face to face and throw dramatic statements like darts, until one of them reaches the denouement: "It's time someone told you, Jessica, after these fifty-seven years, that you're adopted from a tribe of pygmies." Then the speaker turns, as if something meaningful has been accomplished, marches out, and slams the door, leaving us to marvel at these histrionics as poor, shattered—and short—Jessica fades into a commercial.

During that commercial, a dad can refer back to the stunning "slice-of-life" just seen and ask his children what might have happened in *real* life and what a bit of honest listening might have done to improve the outcome. Dramatic but unrealistic behavior seen on TV can be a teaching opportunity. Discussing problems raised in TV dialogue—even though they're often negative examples—can help our children find better ways to handle differences with others.

(Is J.R. Ewing a happy man? Discuss with your children why not.)

Now, although I stated before that it isn't my business to decide which values anyone else should pass on, I do feel strongly about a few key things that I can't resist mentioning.

There are numerous values I want my children to have. Here are a few:

1. LIFE IS GOOD. Young people need the concept that life is good. There is much talk today of even elementary-school children being anxious about nuclear war and of teenagers who are convinced that they won't live to maturity. I hope these young extremists are few in number.

I don't advocate a head-in-the-sand approach. No one past puberty should be unaware of the world's dire potential for destruction. But it worries me a great deal that our youth are often convinced that they will all die young. Such thinking obviously affects everything they do. Some have no college or marriage plans because of their convictions that they won't live through the decade.

A parent can counter this erroneous thinking. It isn't new and has been around for thousands of years. "Eat, drink, and be merry," is a New Testament phrase, "for tomorrow, we die." Young people need hope and the view that life has great potential for joy.

TEACH YOUR CHILDREN, IN A WORD, TO BE OPTIMISTS, EVEN IDEALISTS.

A pessimist reacts to that by saying that realism calls for a dark viewpoint. As a confirmed optimist, I say nonsense to that. I am a total realist in that I know there are disappointments, even that nothing of importance is going to go just as it was planned.

The pessimist lets disappointment keep him from trying. The optimist goes in with his sails fully set, knowing that the set will have to be changed, but that the destination finally arrived at on the far shore will likely be just as good as the original goal. Such a way of looking at life isn't naive; optimism is a function of our attitude toward outcomes.

The world is full of problems; our plans will go awry in many ways, and life can be hard. But life is still good. Point of view makes all the difference. Our children need to know that it's possible to be a realistic idealist.

2. LIFE IS NOW. Young people need to know that, while the future holds much potential, life is right now. Youth tend to want to get through the tenth grade because the eleventh will be better, to get through high school because then they can work or go to college, to always want to get through this to move on to that.

I once read of a man who bought three bottles of expensive champagne at a low price. Knowing little about such things, he put them away for some future grand event. After fifteen years, someone told him that champagne can spoil. That night he opened his champagne.

One of the bottles was barely drinkable. The other two were spoiled. He learned a lesson about waiting too long to begin to live.

HOPE FOR THE FUTURE IS A
GREAT AND MOTIVATING THING,
BUT LIFE IS ALSO RIGHT NOW.

Just because things might be better next year doesn't mean I can't enjoy today. Youth need to be shown the value of doing important things now because the train of life is underway and it only comes down the track once.

3. INTEGRITY OF SOUL. Integrity is a key value for our children to learn. I'm not talking about the basic, obvious kind of honesty—telling the truth and not stealing—which is, of course, vital. I'm talking about integrity of character that makes us whole people.

IT'S RATHER COMMON FOR ADOLESCENTS
TO GROW UP LIVING TWO LIVES.

One life is for parents, church leaders, and teachers. The other is for peers. The first life is polite, honest, obedient, and gives the right answers. The other is rude, often foul-mouthed, disrespectful, and doesn't believe the very answers it spouts. Wearing these two faces may, to some extent, be a natural way of getting along in both the parental and the peer worlds, but this approach can be—at its worst—the pinnacle of cynicism and hypocrisy.

This duplicity is a hard matter to get a handle on, and it afflicts most of us to one degree or another throughout life. But I think it affects teenagers the most and demands attention from a dad.

My father tried to get me to have this kind of integrity when he told me, as a teenager, that if I ever wanted to smoke, to come to him. He would let me make the decision, but he didn't want me to sneak.

Making it clear to children that you understand the problem of pleasing both peers and adults can help them know they aren't the only ones faced with this problem. Though they probably haven't thought of it that way, they can understand that appearing to be something we're not is dishonest.

4. THINKING HELPS. One of the most difficult things to teach, because it's one of the difficult things a thinking person has to do throughout life, is to combine acceptance with skepticism. In our culture, we value both, and, therefore, there's always tension between them.

On the one hand, we're told to obey and accept authority. On the other, we're to think for ourselves and not do those things that don't square with our own consciences. Those two ideas sometimes come into conflict. Often, the contradiction is obvious and therefore easily resolved, such as when an authority figure proposes something that is clearly wrong. But life isn't always that simple.

TEENAGERS SHOULD BE TAUGHT TO THINK FOR THEMSELVES AND TO GIVE THEIR ALLEGIANCE ONLY TO PROVEN THINGS.

People face painful moments in the most serene of lives, but if they understand that individual conscience is primary, they can survive. No one and no organization must be allowed to take free agency from anyone.

While teaching them to question, we can help our children to know that some things do merit their allegiance, and that skepticism as a lifestyle isn't good, either. It's only a tool, not an end in itself.

Another part of this equation is to teach children to question some commonly held values in our society. Surely we ought to teach our children to question some of the following:

—Cutthroat competition. In sports, academics, politics, business, and in other areas, Americans are out to get each other. While competition can be a great motivator, it isn't the only nor the highest value in life.

—Materialism as a way of life. Now, money is a fine thing—one of the finest—in many ways. Not only is it necessary, but our children need to learn to earn and to manage it. But they also need to know that materialism as a way of life has its problems. The consumer mentality is never satisfied. Having a boat isn't enough; with more money, we want a bigger one. Children can learn that materialism is the most "trivial pursuit" of all.

—The rush of modern life. If they can't always take time to smell the roses, they can at least pause and look at them as they go by. We're all busy, but rushing isn't a necessary element of life; it's just an attitude.

The American lifestyle is hurried and harried. Even in leisure, we can't just rest; that appears lazy. Waterskiing is acceptable leisure, because it's busy. Lying in a hammock isn't, because our Puritan forefathers thought it was lazy. Some people rush themselves to death to keep up their active image, when they'd sometimes rather be reading a book under a shade tree.

5. FEELINGS ARE OK. Perhaps the most valuable lesson a child can learn for his personal growth and self-esteem is that all feelings are normal. Whatever he feels, he's allowed to feel. It might not be a "good" feeling, but there is nothing wrong with him for feeling it. What he *does* with what he feels is a different matter. He can't always act out what he feels, except in one way—he's always allowed to *talk* with his parents about what he feels.

Probably all of us have grown up with guilt about some of the things we've felt. But we would be better off if we knew that anger, hate, and envy are just as normal as are love, compassion, and gratitude. Of course, the former are not our ultimate goals, but having "bad" feelings doesn't make us bad.

WE MUST TEACH OUR CHILDREN TO ACCEPT HOW THEY FEEL AND TO DEAL WITH THE FEELINGS, NOT TO PRETEND THEY DON'T EXIST.

To deny your child's feelings—"Now, Johnnie, you don't really hate Billy," when he has just said he does—is to teach Johnnie that he is to feel one thing and say another. In no way does it teach Johnnie not to feel hatred, but just to be a hypocrite about it. By denying the feeling, he makes it impossible to deal with it and rid himself of it.

Teaching our children to trust their feelings and to listen to themselves doesn't guarantee they won't make mistakes, but it puts them on the safest possible course in an unsafe world. The world really is a dangerous place in many, many ways. There are no ideas, people, or concepts that are infallible guides for every situation. But people who trust their own inner feelings of what's right for them—and who combine them with a prayerful effort to do the right thing—are on the safest possible path.

The mention of guilt reminds me of one of the dangers in teaching values. By learning all the things we'd like them to do and be, then by falling short, children can build up a load of guilt to carry around for the rest of their lives.

That isn't healthy or necessary. If we can teach our children to make the best decisions they can and then to get on with life, avoiding the guilt that plagues and drags down so many, they will be mentally healthier. Guilt is a great tool to help us see our errors, but only if it motivates us to do better. When it gets twisted into an end in itself, guilt alone isn't worth anything. It's debilitating, harmful, and crushing to the self-esteem.

One of the findings of modern psychology is that adult happiness doesn't depend on most of what happens in childhood, but it does have a bearing on two things: on the relationship with the same-sex parent and on childhood guilt. The first means that we learn to be productive, happy people by modeling ourselves after our same-sex parent. And, second, that we find happiness only by being free of overwhelming guilt.

Sometimes parents spread guilt with a scoop shovel, and it's crippling influence carries into adulthood. We must teach our children to handle their guilt in a constructive way, a way that improves them, rather than pulls them down.

I've listed a few broad guidelines I want my children to live by. But mainly I want them to be able to be thinkers and adjusters, so they'll be able to carry on when, inevitably, some of the certainties they assumed in their youth to be "gospel" turn to ashes. Life has a way of trying its best to keep us humble.

Topics For Discussion With Your Wife

1. How do we feel about the values we are teaching? How much discrepancy do we feel between what we say and what we do?

2. Are there topics we'd like to role-play with our children? What are our plans for doing so? Which of the other values teaching methods mentioned are we interested in trying right now?

3. Of the broad topics mentioned at the end of this chapter, which ones do we need to strengthen in our children? What other values are we interested in seriously conveying? Which child will we work with first?

4. How much in agreement are we on the ideas in this chapter? Are we working together? Have we identified areas of difference, and are we able to talk about them? Are there major areas we need to discuss further at a future time?

11

Respect for Self
and Others

Any kind of positive relationship with others is predicated on self-respect and acceptance of ourselves. The Bible tells us to ". . .love thy neighbor as thyself." Not a call to egotism, this is rather a clarification of what we might otherwise overlook: a person who has no love of self probably *can't* love anyone else. If I don't care about myself or feel that I'm a worthwhile person, it's possible that I subconsciously think I'm unworthy to love anyone else. Although I say the words and have feelings of love, my own self-rejection constantly interferes with any relationship—husband to wife, parent to child, or neighbor to neighbor. Self-acceptance is the basis of any proper relationship.

This idea is clearly illustrated in the lives of those young adults who, interested in finding marriage partners, yet seem unable to establish a relationship with anyone. Many of them realize that the problem lies within themselves, in their lack of acceptance of self. One young woman put it this way: "Whenever I start to like someone and have hopes for a mutual interest, something very strange happens. If he begins to show any real interest in me, I immediately begin to wonder why. *I say to myself, he couldn't be as good a person as I thought, or he wouldn't like me.* I know this isn't logical. Still it happens every time. And, immediately, the relationship begins to deteriorate."

This becomes a tragic application of Groucho Marx's famous line,

"I wouldn't join any club that would have me for a member."

THOUGH ALL PEOPLE ARE OF WORTH, IF, ON A SUBCONSCIOUS LEVEL, THEY DON'T KNOW IT, THEY FUNCTION AS IF THEY ARE NOT.

By adulthood, patterns of negative self-image are very difficult to change. The time to begin creating good self-esteem in a child is the day he is born.

Dr. Thomas A. Harris taught us in his classic 1969 book, *I'm OK; You're OK*, that there are four basic ways of relating to other people. They are:

1. I'm OK—You're OK
2. I'm OK—You're not OK
3. I'm not OK—You're OK
4. I'm not OK—you're not OK

Only one of these, the number 1 position, is fully healthy. Let's consider the others first, to see what's wrong with them. Number 2 is an egotistical position that says, "I'm a great person, but others aren't. I'm better than anyone else." If we think this way as a parent, we'll talk down to, belittle, shame, and pre-judge our children.

Number 3 is the opposite of number 2. In this case, a person feels, "I'm not as good a person as others are. I'm beneath them." This has nothing to do with true humility. It degrades and belittles the self and is the classic self-esteem problem.

The "sickest" position of all is number 4. Low self-esteem and consequent poor relations with others has led to the attitude, "Not only am I no good, but no one else is, either." This is a sad and cynical view.

"I'M A GOOD PERSON, AND SO ARE YOU," IS THE BASE POSITION FOR TRULY LOVING OURSELVES AND OTHERS.

This position allows us to believe in ourselves and to accept others. We don't look down on people in an egotistical way, nor do we act subservient toward them. We simply accept others as equals.

Very few people are fully consistent in their attitudes. A person may be in the number 1 position with his spouse but in the number 2 spot in his view of his boss. This may seem right because the boss has authority over him, but it's not the ideal attitude. It's possible to be in an equal position in our dealings with a boss and with everyone else.

In very young children, virtually all of their self-image comes from their parents. Whether they feel they're "OK" depends almost entirely on the messages they perceive from mom and dad. They learn whether they're clumsy or coordinated, ugly or cute, dumb or smart, from what their parents tell them. They have, as yet, no ability or opportunity to compare themselves to others. By the time they do—usually when they start school—their self-esteem will already be largely formed.

By this time, children will have learned who they are and whether they're worth much. Most of what they find in school will verify what they've already started to believe about themselves. If they think they're of little worth, school will provide enough negative experiences to give them further evidence. School also provides positive experiences, but these are generally perceived as such only by those who are already on the positive track in their own minds. Throughout life we find what we're programmed to look for.

I don't want to be too negative. There are people who pull themselves up from dreadfully negative upbringings. But how hard it is. Success in later experiences can help but people may never fully overcome the results of negative early home experiences.

Your job, dad, is, first, to be in the number 1 position yourself, then to help your children be there, too. Even in dogs, obsequious servility isn't the goal. And you're not raising dogs. You're raising human beings. Just because they're littler than you are (at first) and know less than you do (at first) doesn't make them less "OK" than you are.

One of the subtle ways we teach our children who they are is through our use of positive labels. Unfortunately, labels also have the power to be extremely destructive to self-esteem.

Humans have a tendency to label and categorize. We like to label in part because labels keep our universe organized and, seemingly, in control. So, once we've labeled, we find unlabeling frustrating. An admission that our universe is not as stable as we had hoped it was isn't pleasant. We don't like to accept the fact that things aren't as simple as our labels had made them seem, or that there's more to a person than we had thought there was. For these reasons, when people change, it isn't easy for us to see the improvement in them.

WHEN SOMEONE BREAKS OUT OF OUR LABELS, IT'S HARD FOR US TO RECOGNIZE, LET ALONE ADMIT.

Suzie's dad fell into this trap when, in the sixth grade, Suzie got off to a poor start with her regular homework assignments. She seldom got it all done and she developed a pattern of not even starting her work until nearly bedtime. Inevitably this pattern caused trouble with Suzie's father. He was concerned not only because she was not getting the work done, but also with her loss of sleep. Discussions with Suzie's teacher verified dad's suspicion that Suzie was often behind in her work, but the teacher added that the problem was no bigger than that of several other students.

"Some students have trouble adjusting to regular homework, but they still come out fine," her teacher said. Rather than pressure her too much, Suzie's parents wisely decided to back off and leave the homework problem to Suzie and the teacher to work out, although mom and dad kept their eye on the matter: a key moment successfully handled.

By the time Suzie was in junior high school she was showing great improvement. Only occasionally was she behind in her work and her teachers had no complaints. But the label remained in dad's mind: "poor at homework." So in parent-teacher conferences—at any hint of less than perfect work on Suzie's part—dad thought, "Oh, that's Suzie, all right; she never did quite get into the homework habit."

Dad's key moments occurred when Suzie came home from school and did everything other than homework. Dad had to decide whether to accuse her of neglecting her work or to leave the matter alone. Most of the time he managed to bite his tongue, but, in his mind, his label kept things simple and clear. Dad had Suzie all figured out.

Unfortunately, his conclusion, being simplistic and based on past events, experiences, and perceptions was simply no longer true. Suzie had fully overcome the original problem.

Dad's label, then, was not only false, but—even if not expressed—was probably damaging to his relationship with his daughter. But, worse, if expressed, the label might actually have hindered her in overcoming the habit fully.

Suzie, like the rest of us, tends to eventually believe the labels she's been given.

Sometimes we decide—we even tell our kids—that they are slow, troublemakers, quarrelers, lazy, or dumb at math. The label is placed, our minds are clear. Now, at any sign of confirmation of our view, we say, "Aha! I was right, wasn't I?" Oh, how we love to be right. So we never let people change. It's a way of keeping them under our control.

IF WE TELL PEOPLE OFTEN ENOUGH THAT THEY ARE LAZY, SLOW, HOT-TEMPERED, OR POOR AT MATH, THEY CAN COME TO BELIEVE US.

Each label comes supplied with a quantity of "Super Glue" that makes it very difficult to remove. When our children try to change, our labels—and their belief in and acceptance of them—won't allow change. Thus we keep our universe in control. We're proven "right," but at what a terrible cost.

Expressions such as, "I'm no good at math," or "I'm clumsy," are signs that the child is starting to label himself as he may have heard others label him. In an adult, these may be no more than honest admissions of weaknesses in areas he has long ago decided aren't of concern to him. In a child, these may be the beginnings of a poor self-image that could intensify to the point of incapacitating him.

Though parents don't always *use* negative terms, they can convey the same negative messages through their sighs, their "Why-do-you-always" questions, their "Oh, come-on" phrases, and other subtleties. Body language may also clearly show impatience or lack of interest. Young people are fast learners. They will get the message, though parents may say they didn't mean to send it.

We've likely all carried with us from childhood a few labels that have helped us and a few that have hurt us. Some of these came from parents and family, and some came from peers. A child labeled by his peers as fat, dumb, ugly, sissy, or teacher's pet, and if he accepts these negative labels, can truly have his life changed. But so can positive labels such as smart, brave, cute, kind, hardworking, and tough change lives. Labels can be positive influences making us want to live up to that quality we've been labeled with:

—"Tommy, you're a good worker."

—"Boy, Joe, I wish I could draw like that; what a talent you have."

—"Suzie, you seem to be doing much better with your homework this year."

I remember fishing with my dad, as a boy, when he complimented on my patience as a fisherman. It hadn't occurred to me that I had any particular patience. I'm not sure I did. But possibly dad had seen a glimmer of it. That I still remember the compliment after all these years indicates that it had a positive effect.

LABELS CAN BE A FORM OF NEGATIVE CONTROL OVER OUR CHILDREN; THEY CAN ALSO BE A LOVING FORM OF POSITIVE REINFORCEMENT WITH LIFE-LONG CONTRIBUTIONS TO SELF-ESTEEM.

Try, consciously, to use labels as tools for good, and watch your children strive to become what you have labeled them.

Let's look at self-image as it relates to sibling relations. With a good self-image a child will have a much better chance of getting along with others. But any family with more than one offspring is going to face squabbles and sibling disputes. And while no parent likes his children to fight, there's a bright side.

BICKERING AND JOCKEYING FOR POSITION AMONG SIBLINGS OFTEN TEACHES THEM INSIGHTS INTO LIFE.

Through "sibling interaction" (it sounds better than "fighting," doesn't it?) young people learn more about who they are and how their actions and views affect the lives of others. They also learn about sharing and considering the feelings of others.   (That is, they learn these things if we can keep them from murdering each other first.)

Though children learn from interacting with their siblings, I'm not suggesting that we leave them entirely to their own battles. Some children are more aggressive in pursuing their desires than others, and you may have to save one from another now and then—and not always is it the smaller one that needs the life rope. If you see a pattern developing, say of harshness to younger brothers or sisters, you have the duty to talk to the offender. But in private, where possible.

Reducing sibling collisions in the first place is partly up to you, dad. First, we should be careful not to set up a competitive atmosphere between siblings. There must be no open comparing of one child to another. Each child must be allowed to be unique. Jimmy may keep a neater room, but younger Johnny may have reason for less neatness. He may have more interests, more junk (hand-me-downs from Jimmy), and prefer more variety in his activities, all of which contribute to a messier room. And let's not forget that neat Jimmy may be a compulsive cleaner, which, if carried to the extreme, is just as neurotic as a compulsive "junker." Work on Johnny to clean his room if you need to, but don't do it by comparing his mess to Jimmy's hallowed floor.

Rather than as competitors, children should think of family members as members of a team, a special team that wouldn't be the same without each one. An attitude of helping one another and contributing to the whole is the proper one. The day a child volunteers to do a chore for another who is in a hurry to get someplace is the day a parent feels a little success.

Perhaps the main sibling values to foster are respect and forgiveness: a spirit of overlooking the small stuff and forgiving the big stuff.

If we can apply the same concepts to our children that we apply to our adult friends, sibling relations may be held to a low roar. And, occasionally, we will see moments of real love and concern. One poignant moment occurred at our house when Geneal was small, to indicate her love of her older sister.

She said, "Dad, I cleaned Angela's room." I asked why and she said, "Because she didn't make any noise when I told a story in home evening."

A dad needs to consider the role of his children's friends in building their self-esteem. At some points, especially around the midteens, those friends will be a lot more influential in daily decisions than you will be, dad. Pray that your children will have good friends.

IT'S VITAL THAT EACH OF YOUR CHILDREN HAS A GOOD FRIEND.

Your child may or may not have lots of friends—that doesn't particularly matter—but he needs one "best" friend who accepts him as he is. If your child doesn't have a best friend, a parent can encourage after-school contacts. You may suggest sleep-overs and other activities to some of your children who may be shy about making these arrangements themselves.

Try to get to know your children's friends and let them know they're welcome at your house. You thereby communicate to your child that he is a person of worth—an equal with a right to bring his friends home.

In the unenviable case that your child has chosen friends you don't approve of, handle this key moment very carefully. The general rule is that you don't have to accept all of your children's friends *in your home* but you do have to let your children choose their own friends.

If you do have concerns about his choice of friends, be candid with your child. Tell him just what it is that worries you about his friend. Young people are sensitive to fairness and justice. They will assume, unless you tell them otherwise, that you are rejecting their friends because of skin color, hair style, differences in social standing, or other externals.

Sit down and say, "It's not Jack's orange punk hair that bothers me, son; it's his smoking. I don't reject him for that either, but I worry that you might pick up the habit."

Just don't get into the trap of telling a child whom he can be friends with. It's like telling him he can't like peanut butter. You can't control what or whom he likes. If you try, he will quickly prove that point. You can only apply guidelines and restrictions. But caution is in order because of the danger of giving the wrong message to your child, including the one that says, "If you don't like my friends, you don't like me."

Respecting your children and treating them as equals (position 1 on the "OK-scale") doesn't mean giving in to their views (position 3) any more than it means forcing them to bend to yours (position 2). A whole household of strong-willed position 1 people can get along just fine if they know a few interpersonal skills. Not tricks or manipulation tools, these basic skills help us to find out what others feel and to communicate what we feel, so that everyone can get more of what he wants.

THE BASIS OF SUCH HUMAN RELATIONS SKILLS IS THAT EVERYONE IS TREATED AS AN EQUAL, DESERVING OF OUR RESPECT AND INTEREST.

Communicating equality works wonders. Many times when I've argued with a child, I've suddenly recognized the key moment and stopped to say, "Let's start over. I don't mean to put you down. I really want to know how you feel." The results from this approach are very different from the defensive position I had been forcing my child into. Often I hadn't understood fully what he was saying. Therefore, we were arguing over the wrong thing entirely.

But how do we treat people as equals? How do we get them to feel free to say what they feel? How do we dare say what we feel? These things require two basic skills: listening and leveling.

I. LISTENING. The first skill is non-judgmental listening. Wonders can be accomplished when we give real attention to what our kids say. But it takes practice not to be a bored, defensive, selective listener, or an interrupter. When your child says to you, "I can't stand my teacher; she's the worst teacher I've ever had," your reaction is likely to be either negative or positive. However, "Oh, she is not; if you'd study you wouldn't have any problem," or "Yes, your sister didn't like her, either," does nothing but start an argument or end a conversation.

You don't really know what is being said, do you? Your child's statement could mean nearly anything. Yet, you've made a judgment by agreeing or disagreeing.

What else is there, you ask? Well, there's finding out more about what's being said. That is where non-judgmental listening comes in.

Since your child probably has some emotion behind his statement, it may be very important that you determine his real message. Instead of making a judgment just yet, we can recognize the key moment and say something like one of the following:

—"Tell me more," (an open non-judgmental invitation)

—"You seem to feel strongly about this," (reflecting feelings)

—"You feel you have a poor teacher?" (reflecting content).

These are non-judgmental statements intended to solicit more information, or, often more important, to allow the other person to get past his anger, or other emotion, by venting it on your willing ear. Once he does that, you may find out what he's really saying, and he may be able to talk about it more calmly.

Listening is hard, at first, but, with practice, works wonderfully well.

II. LEVELING. The second basic skill is leveling, which is, in some ways, the reverse of listening. When a person comes to you with a strong statement, you use listening. When *you* are the one with the strong feelings, you use leveling.

Leveling replaces the fighting, attacking, and blaming we often use to make our statements. But leveling is more than simply "nice" talking—the discussion can be very direct without attacking or making the problem worse.

Suppose you come home from work one summer day and find the lawn unmowed after your son promised he would mow it before he went to afternoon football practice. When he comes back from practice, and you face your key moment, what is your usual response, especially if you feel your son is getting away with something?

My natural response is to attack, send him to mow before he eats, and to feel I'm teaching him a good lesson. But, while the lawn may get mowed, I may have created a new problem in the way I handled it.

Leveling is a way of stating feelings without blaming and without making the problem worse. Here's how it might sound: "Son, I need to talk with you a minute. I'm feeling very angry right now, because I feel a promise was broken. I want to get this settled."

Notice that the feelings were expressed without accusations. You stated how *you* felt, not what *he* did or didn't do. But it isn't a "sissy" way of talking; it's an honest, straightforward approach that let's you say what you think and therefore get it off your chest and start feeling better right away—but not at your son's expense. Because he is treated as an equal, your son doesn't have to feel worse just so you can feel better.

If your son's answer is that the lawn mower broke and he spent as much time as he had trying to fix it, then you'll be glad you used a decent approach, won't you? If he says he forgot, you may still send him out to mow before dinner, but he will more than likely feel that you've been fair because you've merely enforced the original agreement rather than attacking his motives or his character.

Psychologists tell us that males in our culture have trouble sharing their feelings, especially in the presence of women. So it may take effort for dads to get to the point of being able to listen and especially to level. But these communication skills work much better than the extreme of throwing dishes or the other extreme of pretending we aren't upset (a misguided application of Christian principles, in my opinion). And you may be surprised at how clearly young people see their responsibilities and commitments if they're approached in a manner that treats them as other adults would be treated. A position based on respect for the views of others leaves no losers.

(Source for the concept of leveling is C. Kay Allen, *The Journey From Fear To Love,* Human Values Institute, 6 Abilene St., Aurora, Colorado, 80011. Used by permission.)

Topics For Discussion With Your Wife

1. How do we feel about our children's acceptance of themselves as worthy people? Is there one of them who needs our special attention with self-esteem at this time?
2. In what position is each of our children on the "I'm OK—You're OK" chart? What position are we in? If we're not all in position number 1, how can we help one another get there?
3. What kinds of labels do we use in our home? How could we use positive ones to help our children grow?

4. How do we feel about our children's sibling relations? Are there things we need to do to improve this situation?

5. Does each of our children have a good friend at the moment? Need we intercede in any current friendship in any way? Do our children feel that we accept their friends?

6. Is the non-judgmental listening skill a natural response at our house? If not, do we want to make it so?

7. How are feelings expressed in our house? Is leveling, or something similar, a better possibility than our present approach?

8. How much in agreement are we on the ideas in this chapter? Are we working together? Have we identified areas of difference, and are we able to talk about them? Are there major areas we need to discuss further at a future time?

12

Conflicting Needs

Children grow and mature every day and become better able to handle greater responsibility, but some of us don't very easily adjust our treatment of them. We hold on to our children for two reasons: one is our fear that they will fail without us; the other is that we like the feeling of control over them.

There's nothing sinister in the fact that we like to be able to control our children. It's a natural, "parent" feeling. But as natural as it is, parental control runs right up against an opposite natural feeling, this one in the child: the desire and need for independence.

CHILDREN MUST GET FREE; IT'S PART OF THEIR NATURE. BUT PARENTS DON'T LIKE TO LET GO; THAT'S PART OF THEIR NATURE.

And that's where the problems start. It's like two freight trains heading toward one another on the same track. Catastrophe is a certainty unless someone does something about it.

Sometimes parents fail to see the other train coming. Until a confrontation arises that forces parents to see the problem, they still treat their sixteen-year-old like the six-year-old she used to be. Though not all sixteen-year-olds rebel outwardly, this approach has a terrible cost in terms of proper development into adults.

Certainly there are reins on both of these drives. Not every teenager feels he's ready right now to get free, nor is every parent anxious to keep his children at home forever. But the basic drives are still present.

Some parents still refuse to see that their teenagers can have a point of view, however. A young bride was leading a group of adults in a church class and referred to the idea that our children are, in a sense, only loaned to us, for a time, so that we can teach them and send them out on their own.

An old man stood and said, "Young lady, my children are not loaned to me. They are given to me. They are just as much my possessions as are my house, my land, or my car. I am totally responsible for them."

Momentarily overwhelmed and doubtful of her position, the young woman felt embarrassed and had no argument. Years went by before she decided she had been right all along.

Although common in earlier times, most of us would find this man's view and its implications extreme indeed. Yet, some of our actions toward our children may indicate that deep down, we subscribe to the view that we own our children or that we are totally responsible for them.

Recognition of the opposing drives helps explain many difficulties we encounter with teenagers. Explaining this view *to them* is the next step. They also need to understand what's happening. Both of you must accept that tensions are likely to result from these two conflicting drives. But as long as parents and children are willing to recognize the other's needs, they can talk through problems. So we must keep communicating. Here are two big ways to do so.

1. GET TO KNOW YOUR CHILDREN'S VIEWS. One way to communicate is to wait until a problem develops. This is storm-troop negotiating, and you're bound to experience some of it. Some problems can't be anticipated, so you need to handle them as they arise.

A better way is to talk, where possible, about concepts in advance, when no trouble is brewing. Which style prevails at your house—stormtroop or advance talking—depends on your temperament and that of your children. Though I disagree, there are those who don't like the advance approach because they find it a waste of time to talk without a specific problem at hand.

Open-ended items (similar to those in chapter 5 under interviewing) help you learn how your children feel about themselves and their relation to the family. The only requisite is starting with an attitude that diversity is acceptable. If you feel your offspring have to agree with you on everything, skip this activity.

Read to your child statement number 1 below (or create your own items) and have your child mark the degree, from 0 to 10, to which he agrees. "Not at all" is a 0; "fully" is a 10. He can mark any spot in between.

You should also mark a paper with your rating of that item. Read off all the items you feel would be appropriate, and add your own at the end. Then compare the two sheets and discuss the items you wish, especially those where your ratings differ greatly from those of your child.

Here's the list: (Substitute your child's name for "Jim." It's repetitive to use the child's name in nearly every item, but the use makes him remember that we're talking about his own specific relationship with you, not vague generalities.)

1. Jim is ready to handle life.
2. Jim's parents have a right to direct his life.
3. Jim's parents have experience and wisdom beyond his.
4. Jim's parents might know him better in some ways than he knows himself.
5. Communicating true feelings is difficult and takes a lot of time.
6. Jim is willing to spend the time it takes to do this communicating.
7. Jim's parents are too strict with him.
8. "That's how I am" is sufficient reason for a person to stay how he is.
9. Reason and discussion are ways to solve disputes.
10. The overall parent/Jim relationship is pretty good right now.
11. The parent/Jim relationship is on an upward swing.
12. Jim's parents understand him.
13. Jim's parents trust him.
14. Jim is doing his part at home and with his overall contribution to the family.
15. Any problems between Jim and his parents can be fixed by a change in the parents' attitudes alone.
16. It should be up to Jim, alone, to set the time he comes in,

and to determine other rules of behavior.

17. The parent/Jim relationship is better than the parent/child relationship in other homes.

18. For Jim, friends are a good source of information and advice on daily decisions.

19. Parents are a good source of information and advice on daily decisions.

20. Friends are a good source of information and advice on big decisions.

21. Parents are a good source of information and advice on big decisions.

22. Jim sees parental rules as guidelines, to be broken when it seems necessary.

23. Jim's parents see the rules as hard and fast, never to be broken.

24. Jim is mature enough to be given total freedom.

25. Jim feels his parents are willing to give him more freedom.

26. Jim feels he could be entirely open with his parents.

27. Jim feels it's important to obey parental rules, even when they seem unfair.

28. Jim is flexible and adaptable.

29. Jim's parents are flexible and adaptable.

30. In spite of disagreements and rules, Jim is always certain his parents love him.

Don't use any items you don't feel good about. And don't make your child respond to items he wants to skip.

Be prepared, dad, for possible feelings of being misunderstood. Your wisdom and understanding, that you marked so high, may be marked a little lower by your less observant child. This might be a key moment so don't be defensive. Don't try to prove, or convince. Just talk.

DADS HAVE TO TAKE A LITTLE ABUSE SOMETIMES. YOU WON'T BE THOUGHT OF IN JUST THE WAY YOU WANT TO BE NO MATTER WHAT YOU DO.

If people don't see you in the way you want them to, keep in mind this interesting statistic (which I can't verify): In the 1980 presidential campaign, 80 percent of Reagan's supporters felt that the press was pro-Carter while 80 percent of Carter's supporters felt that the press was pro-Reagan.

You may often feel that way as a dad. But don't let lack of recognition get you down. Do the best you can and leave it at that. Your reward will come in a different way—in the good lives of your children, when they're adults, and your responsibility for them is finished.

2. RECOGNIZE DIFFERENT MATURITY LEVELS. Sometimes we forget that it takes a long time to become an adult, and that growth can't be rushed too much.

IN DEALING WITH OUR CHILDREN WE HAVE TO REMEMBER THAT THEY ARE ON A DIFFERENT MATURITY LEVEL.

Realize that moral development seems to follow routine steps as does learning to read or to walk. If a child isn't performing on the level you think he should be on, perhaps he doesn't know how to do so yet. The growth steps to put him where you want him to be haven't been made.

Theories about moral development are interesting. But the trouble with detailing them here is that psychologists disagree on many points: what to call the levels or steps, how certain it is that everyone follows them, whether a person can be hurried in his movement to the next step, what is the average age of attainment of the next step, whether one level is higher than another, and why some sixty-year-olds don't seem to have developed beyond where most twelve-year-olds are. Interesting as these models are, there is too much disagreement in professional circles to warrant using them in raising your children.

However, there is one simple, three-step development chart that might be instructive. It can help us in seeing why we might have problems with our children, and can't figure out "where they're at."

Level 1 seems to run from birth until about the age of eight. In this era decisions are made mostly in one's own interests, with the fear of punishment for wrong-doing a prime factor in an eventual decision.

From about eight to twelve years of age is level 2. This is the age of law and order, when a child likes to see fairness and justice prevail. He isn't as concerned with punishment and reward as he was. He feels that, if he does the right thing, fairness will be its own reward. He's moved beyond demanding what he wants all the time to often thinking about what is best for the group, especially about what is fair and just, and what maintains order. He likes to know the rules.

Level 3 begins at about age twelve and continues into adulthood. This level is more self-directed, with worry not so much about what's fair for the group as about what's right for the person's own conscience. Principles are sought more than rules—principles to provide guidance in varying situations. Level 3 people realize that there aren't enough rules to cover every situation in advance.

This is a simplified way of looking at moral development and the three levels can't be seen with certainty in every decision a child makes. Still, they are useful guidelines to use so we don't demand that children react as adults before they are able.

A move to the next level doesn't mean a child leaves the last one entirely behind. Not even all "adult" decisions are made at level 3.

I've known of adult church leaders who saw no reason for lateness to an evening training meeting *ever*, including once when a car pool group had to traverse miles of freeway in a blinding blizzard. Even to go out in that weather was lunacy; arrival at all was questionable for this out-of-town group; arrival on time was impossible. But a level 2 leader publicly chastised them anyway.

Most family rules are at level 2, aren't they? (The idea of rules is, in the first place, a level two idea, I suspect.) We teach our children to come in on time, to do their chores, to keep up on homework, and to live an orderly, rule-bound life. There's nothing wrong with that. Much of the world's day-to-day business wouldn't get done without such an orientation. But level 2 isn't the only viewpoint.

WE FRUSTRATE OUR TEENAGERS

GREATLY WHEN WE INSIST THAT THEY FOLLOW THE RULES— STAY AT LEVEL 2—IN EVERY SITUATION.

Bill might decide to stay an hour later at the party because a video was late getting started. That's a level 3 decision; he's thought it through and applied a principle: since he came to see the movie, why miss the last hour?

But when sixteen-year old Bill makes that level 3 decision, and his forty-five-year old dad is operating on level 2 about arrival times, watch out! When Bill comes in late, dad grounds him for six years for breaking the rule—a level 2 application. (Notice I didn't say dad was wrong in being concerned, just that he and Bill are operating on different levels.)

Yet, if Bill had been hurrying to get home on time and the little red "oil" light lit up on the dashboard, dad would expect him to make a level 3 decision: stop the car, and call for help, even if it meant getting home late. Chastisement is too weak a word to describe what dad would do to him if Bill said, "Dad, I knew that you were a law-and-order, level-2 man, and that the only important thing was to get home on time. Sorry about the engine."

We're often inconsistent ourselves in what we expect as well as in what we do. Therefore, we can't make these levels too binding. A dad can afford a bit of flexibility in where he and his children are on the scale.

Recognizing conflicting needs and maturity levels between yourself and your children will help in many ways. Don't underestimate your kids, and continue to push them to higher levels, but don't demand that they see everything your way. Give them time.

Topics For Discussion With Your Wife

1. How much in agreement are we with the idea that there are conflicting needs in parents and teenagers? Does knowing this help? Would talking to our children about it help?

2. How do we feel about using the open-ended rating approach in

getting to know our children?

3. How do we feel about tolerating a little abuse in the way our children think about us? What do we feel is important for them to know about us?

4. How do we feel about the moral development of our children in relation to ourselves? Does that explain some of the difficulties we may have had?

5. How much in agreement are we on the ideas in this chapter? Are we working together? Have we identified areas of difference, and are we able to talk about them? Are there major areas we need to discuss further at a future time?

13

Discipline

The most important thing to be said about discipline is a very serious thing, indeed: if you're abusive, get help.

It's one thing to get upset, as parents do, and even to let your emotions come out in the standard forms. It's quite another to lose control so that you go beyond the bounds of standard, acceptable discipline practices with your children. That is a failed key moment of the most frightening kind.

EXCEPT FOR PRISONS, OUR HOMES ARE THE MOST VIOLENT INSTITUTIONS IN AMERICA.

That's a sobering fact. And, although physical abuse isn't the only kind, it's the type with the greatest potential for immediate, serious harm. If you're a person with a "short fuse" who starts hitting and finds that one blow leads to another, you need outside help before this happens again. How much better that *you* recognize the problem and seek a solution than that someone else have to intervene or, worse, that you do real harm to one of your family members.

Abuse also includes excesses other than physical harm. The less obvious kind of abuse is the emotional control that some like to exert. Abuse of this type is harder to prove; it can pass for concern and a desire to guide our families. But, while outsiders might not be able to judge, *you* can probably sense when it has reached the point that your rules and demands are so excessive that failure on the part of the children is nearly certain. This is a sign that you've set up an increasingly impossible system to live by, and you need to face the question of why you've felt compelled to do this. This is apparently a form of control that benefits *you* in some psychological way, rather than the children.

IN EITHER OF THESE TYPES OF ABUSE, PLEASE GET HELP FROM YOUR SPOUSE, A CHURCH LEADER, FRIEND, OR COUNSELOR.

If abuse is happening at your house, face it. Don't fool yourself into thinking that it isn't happening or hide behind the false idea that only crazies abuse their families. Various kinds of poor behavior can come from any of us, and because child abuse has such enormous potential for large scale and long-term physical and emotional damage, it's imperative that help be obtained right away.

All of us, even non-abusers, can find ourselves in a situation now and then where our temper has flared and we're berating one or more of our children. When this happens, sometimes our "righteous rage" causes us to continue too long or be otherwise excessive, especially where our child is responding in unsuitable ways rather than showing the good sense to humbly submit to our wisdom.

Here are three suggestions for handling your anger. First, work out with your wife an acceptable way to "interfere" to help you get back in control, if you happen to fail at the key moment yourself. Do the same for her. This generally has to be worked out in advance because, in the heat of the moment, no one likes someone else cutting in. So a pre-arranged signal or comment can be a boon.

Second, pre-determine what the big problems are for you, those things that really bother you, so that you can think through how to handle them better. The one that bothers me the most is cheekiness. My kids know cheekiness is the way to get dad riled, so they use it only when they are very upset themselves or when they're feeling especially reckless. Since I recognize my short fuse on this matter, I'm better able to deal with it.

Third, the old advice of counting to ten isn't bad in that it allows us to cool down a little before dealing with the issue. Incidentally, research shows that the difference between the abuser and the standard parent may be in just this one area: the abuser seems to have no delayed fuse, and moves more quickly into the rage that the standard parent has learned to postpone long enough to reduce.

Now that we've covered the dangers of excess, let's talk about discipline as a positive tool in helping our children develop. The fact is that, in spite of our greatest efforts to produce love, harmony, and cooperation in our homes, in spite of one-to-one listening, leveling, and participative attitudes with our children, there are going to be times when they will go against our parental ideas of proper behavior, and we find ourselves needing to teach them the error of their ways. That's what discipline is for.

There are several points to keep in mind.

1. DISCIPLINE SHOULD COMMUNICATE LOVE. It must be clear to all in the family that discipline isn't synonymous with punishment. Punishment implies retribution, getting even, and revenge; discipline, in the broadest sense, is to teach, to instill self-control and to improve future behavior, and has a caring component. Punishment looks to the past; discipline to the future. A young child doesn't always see much difference here. Being disciplined and being punished might be the same thing to him. But in your own motives, you must always know the difference.

Discipline needs follow-up to show concern, praise, and love. No one expects a judge, who is only doing his job when he sentences a man, to go to the prison to put his arms around the prisoner. No one expects the drill sergeant, who is also only doing his job, to console a private he has "sentenced" to extra night patrol for a poorly-made bed.

BUT YOU'RE NOT A JUDGE AND YOU'RE NOT A DRILL SERGEANT. YOU'RE A DAD, AND IT'S YOUR JOB TO LOVE.

It doesn't weaken your position in the least to give extra love to a child who has missed dinner. If you see your role as mean guy who must play it tough for some reason, you're actually inflicting double punishment on the child: missing out on dinner and missing out on dad's love.

When you change your view of your role to teacher and "administrator of consequences," it actually strengthens your position to show an increased love to a child who is paying the price for her infraction. A key moment comes when you realize that it's at this very instant when she needs your love the most. If she seems to reject your offering, it's because she's angry, not because she doesn't need your support.

God isn't a bad guy because he lets us suffer the consequences of our actions. Neither are you a bad guy when you let your child learn in this way. But just in case there's any doubt about that in the mind of that child, talk about what's happened, be sure she understands the rule and the consequences, praise her, where possible, for handling it well, and leave a hug or two.

The biggest problem with discipline in relation to self-esteem is that the child thinks she is "bad" for having broken the rule. If you will show love in your discipline, you can help counter that feeling of rejection and failure.

Though discipline is necessary, it does have its long-range danger—according to how it's interpreted by the child. A University of Tennessee study indicated that a child's self-esteem is harmed by punishment. Since discipline—even in the best sense of loving instruction—is likely, in the eyes of a child, to carry a component of punishment, its potential for damaging self-esteem must be kept in mind.

2. DISCIPLINE HAS TO MAKE SENSE. Ideally, the consequences of rule breaking are natural ones arising out of the incident itself. If a child is late to dinner without good cause, in a household where the rule is that all eat together, he has clearly missed eating. No one needs to send him to his room or ground him if he's hungry but finds no dinner. The consequence is perfectly natural and "punishing" in itself.

If a child stays up too late but still has to get up on time, his tiredness is another natural consequence. There are numerous other cases where natural, automatic consequences become the means of discipline. If we will let life work for us as often as possible, we will teach more about life than about punishment.

3. WE DON'T OWN ANYONE. Ultimately we are not responsible for our child's choices. Each person is his own master.

PART OF THE RAGE WE SOMETIMES FEEL WHEN SOMEONE DISOBEYS US COMES FROM OUR FEELING OF LACK OF CONTROL OVER THIS PERSON.

When we can recognize that we are responsible only for our own actions, not for those of others, we are better off—and so are our families. The ideal is to let children make their choices and let the consequences follow, so that they will learn as we once had to.

4. AVOID EXCESSIVE OR MEANINGLESS DEMANDS. Discipline should include no manipulation, trickery, or excessive control, and should be built on respect for our children. Sometimes the attitude that we're responsible leads us to try to manipulate people to our way of doing things. We purport that the rules are for the good of our children, but often there is no obvious way to show that that's the case.

Excessive control can result from trying to apply out-dated rules or rules that make no sense to anyone but you. I heard of one man who wouldn't allow channel-switching during commercials on TV because he felt it immoral to "cheat" the companies providing the programs. I suspect that this type of behavior is done to fulfill some need in the father rather than to help his children.

Repeated discipline over the same offenses may be more a problem with a system that demands too much than with the child.

We moved our dinner time to accommodate the delivery of afternoon newspapers by our children. Actually, when they hurried, they could make it on time. But it put on a lot of needless pressure, and it seemed simpler just to move the dinner back a bit. Unless it's an absolutely critical item, there's little point in forcing a child to repeatedly break himself against the rule.

Discipline isn't for proving anything. Some parents seem to make demands just to show that they are in charge. A clash of wills is the frequent result. Dad wants to be the boss; his kids want to show him he's not. Dad might "win" at the moment but it's a win sown with the seeds of future crop failure.

DISCIPLINE ISN'T FOR PARENTS TO PROVE ANYTHING OR TO BE ANYTHING. IT ISN'T TO FILL ANY PARENTAL NEEDS WHATSOEVER.

Discipline mustn't become an end in itself. When it's too excessive or too frequent, discipline begins to lose its effectiveness as a teacher. Kids then pay more attention to how to avoid the discipline than they do to learning the lessons the discipline was supposed to teach. If you find yourself disciplining constantly, you will need to stop and take a harder look at the system.

5. BE REASONABLE, NEGOTIATE, COMPROMISE. Remember that there are sometimes mitigating circumstances. Your role as administrator of consequences in your household doesn't make you a cold-blooded executioner. A dad must always be willing to listen to his child's view. If you find that he's merely making excuses to get out of the consequences, talk with him about that, and get on with the discipline. On some occasions, though, he will have valid reasons for his actions, and, in those cases, don't be afraid to waive the consequences. Even in cases of reasonable doubt, it's better, in my opinion, to say, "OK—this time." Demonstrate reason.

It's been suggested that, as parents, we negotiate while we still can. When your child is ten years old, you don't really need to negotiate. You can just force your will (not, however, without future consequences, I would suggest). But when he is twenty, if you've forced your will too often, you may push too hard and find him gone.

SOMEWHERE IN THOSE TEN YEARS YOU NEEDED TO LEARN A LITTLE GIVE AND TAKE SO THAT HE FELT HE HAD SOME SAY IN THE RULES.

When he's twenty, unless he's physically or mentally disabled, you have no more negotiating power than he wants to give you: he can just walk away and move out.

If you say, "Let him go, then," you miss my point. It's one thing to have to make a difficult, rational decision to move a disruptive child to a different environment, but no child ought to have to move out of your home because of a confrontation. That's failed parenting.

When we negotiate while we still have authority to do so, we don't abdicate; we merely recognize that rules that apply to a ten-year-old might not all have to apply to a twenty-year-old.

(Don't construe any of this to imply that a twenty-year old doesn't have to follow certain requirements while he's under your roof. He does, just as any adult does, just as you do. It's just that he might be allowed a more adult set of rules than those required of him as a child.)

Though it isn't *always* a good solution, compromise is a handy item to have in your communication-skills pack. But there are dads who won't use compromise. They feel it shows weakness to give in a little. I hope your children don't have a dad who is so unrealistic.

If you always treat rules as unbreakable, you're not demonstrating understanding which may create resentment. When you insist on unbending exactness in every situation, you make clear that rules are more important to you than people.

6. MATCH THE DISCIPLINE TO THE INFRACTION. Playing the radio too loudly doesn't equate with coming in drunk at 4 a.m. Yet parents sometimes weight all infractions the same in the severity of the lecture given. After the lecture makes us feel better, we ought to try to match the punishment to the crime—unless the lecture itself is sufficient.

(I'm convinced there's a pulpit-pounding preacher in most of us dads if you get us on the right topic. But try to save your sermons for a more appreciative audience than your bored children. I finally learned that most of my long homilies—logical, convincing, and lovely though I thought them to be—were less for teaching my children than for being sure I was logical, clear, and "right." My polemics were only filling my own needs.)

I suggest a three-tiered scale for determining the level of infractions:
—Be tough with willful, deliberate breaking of rules. Defiance is serious.
—Deal less harshly with slovenly attention to rules. Carelessness needs instruction.
—Deal not at all with accidents. I don't have to tell you, of course, that if the same infraction happens too often, it *isn't* an accident.

Adolescents are going to test the rules just as surely as drying prunes are going to wrinkle. Teenagers are part of nature's plan to bug us. But adolescents need more "space" than do younger children. A wise dad will decide to overlook or say little about certain things.

I'm convinced that much of what teenagers demand is merely the chance to try things their way. They like to be their own persons. When Angela first asked to skydive, I put her off, hoping she would forget about it. When a year later, at 17, she was still determined, I signed her permission slip—with a shaky hand.

In our efforts to determine what needs attention and what doesn't, it helps to try to predict the future consequences of a given behavior.

NOTE THAT WHAT MANY PARENTS LABEL AS BIG PROBLEMS ARE LABELED SMALL ONES BY PSYCHOLOGISTS.

The most serious behavioral problems are *not* contradicting elders, disrespect, impertinence, or rudeness. Those—in tolerable moderation—are signs of a healthy personality testing boundaries. Though we needn't tolerate insolence, we needn't get too alarmed about it, either. This testing is vital and basic to growth. The *real* problems, incidentally, from a psychological point of view, are unsociableness, suspiciousness, withdrawal, and paranoia.

7. ALL SHOULD CONTRIBUTE TO THE RULE-MAKING PROCESS. Children often feel compelled to break the rules. They will feel this need less if they have had a hand in helping make the rules in the first place. Remember what the Coopersmith study found: a democratic home contributes to self-esteem.

You may be the head administrator in your family, but, without input from the rest of the family into the system, you will be seen as an unfair despot. People can love a despot, but they can't like him, and they can't trust him. Despotism teaches children that discipline is arbitrary, uncertain, and whimsical, rather than swift, sure, and fair. Then they start to pay more attention to dad's mood than to learning to follow the rules for the right reasons.

The idea of partnership doesn't have to imply complete agreement on everything. Sometimes we hear advice that parents have to be in total agreement on all matters. Forget that. You can teach a valuable lesson about participative leadership by talking about discipline matters with your wife *and* with the children. You teach lessons about compromise, cooperation, and negotiation by showing that conclusions and decisions are reached and supported by all—after everyone has had a chance for input.

8. CATEGORIZE PROBLEMS. Children can be corrected so often that they feel personally picked on. This is harmful to the parent-child relationship. What might be happening, though, to get dad's attention so often, is that the same problem is recurring and you find yourself coming down on the same thing over and over.

Sitting down to think through recent infractions might help you find a pattern. When I've done this, I've been able to go to a child and say, "Look, I know you think I jump on you for everything. But I've looked at what has bothered me in the last week and found only two or three categories. Would you like to hear them?"

Once the child sees that you are having a problem, say, with his coming to dinner late and selfish behavior toward his siblings, he can see these as manageable problems. I would also point out to him, in this key moment, that in many, many other areas, you are very proud of him and happy with his behavior. Encourage him to work on problems you've categorized and let him know when you notice improvement.

9. "I TOLD YOU SO'S" HAVE A PLACE. Nobody likes to hear "I told you so. . ." Especially my wife, who can sense one coming in a simple clearing of the throat or a "Well. . ." "Don't say it," she says.

In walking up to someone and smugly spouting, "I told you so," I agree with her completely. But in defense of those of us who can't let a teaching moment pass, let me state my opinion that there is a way to say "I told you so" that isn't offensive. More to the point, there's a *reason* to say it that is valid, beyond the ego-related one that can be so obnoxious.

Suppose you've suggested to your young son that he save the five dollars he's been carrying around because he will probably want to spend it on something over the Christmas holidays. He doesn't heed you and buys something with it. When his buddy asks him to go bowling and to a movie over the holidays, your son is disappointed that he has no money.

Now if you leave it at that, a ten-year old might or might not get the point. But since you're sure this type of thing is bound to come up again, you find it acceptable to discuss with him the decision he made.

In the strictest sense, it's an "I told you so," without using those words and without the arrogant tone. But if you can help your boy see how he got himself into the problem and what he might do to improve the situation in the future, an "I told you so" is worth the risk.

10. BE PREPARED. When a problem does arise, here are some specifics—

—Acknowledge the problem. There are people who seem unwilling to admit that a conflict exists. Sometimes this is because they were raised with the idea that conflict *shouldn't* exist. The longer we put off the acknowledgment, the bigger the problem can grow. If it's truly one of those problems that will shrivel and die with benign neglect, fine. There are some things best ignored. But if it's a recurring matter, acknowledge it while it's still tiny.

—Be sure you communicate caring, not rejection. It's easy for a child to feel rejected when you discuss concerns about behavior. The best way to see that this impression is not conveyed is to say so. "I hope you don't think I'm rejecting you, son," is a fine start. "I'm just worried about this particular problem."

—Don't interrogate. Get information as you go along, not in a burst of questions which can put anyone on the defensive—especially if there's a hint that you doubt the answers or distrust the motives expressed.

—Stick to the real issues. Some teenagers are experts at maneuvering. Deal with the problem, not the side problems. ("That's a matter we might need to discuss at another time, Mark, but not until we finish the issue at hand.") Don't succumb to clever reversals, either. ("You may be right that your brother gets away with the same thing, and I would be willing to discuss that with you later. But right now, we're talking about you.")

Sticking to the issues will tend to keep the discussion short enough to fit into a normal two-day weekend, too. Personally, I love long tautologies. Just ask my wife. But my children don't, so the results are generally counterproductive.

—Breathers may be necessary to relieve tension in a serious discussion. There comes a point when it helps to say, "Let's finish this later." The pause will give you both time to regroup and consider what the real issues are. After the problem is clarified, you could come back in a *second* session to talk about disciplinary action that might be necessary.

—Timing is critical. If possible, find a time suitable for both of you. If you force a child to talk when he's late or worried about something else, you will distort his responses and probably increase his hostility.

—Avoid provoking. Try to avoid accusations or statements that make matters worse. ("You always . . .") Don't broaden the charges unless what you're bringing in is critical to the discussion. ("You never cared about. . .")

In light of the above guidelines, I believe there are two types of discipline approaches.

I. FLARE-UPS. Flare-ups occur when a child violates your expectations and requires an immediate response. The definition of a flare-up situation is that there are no rules or consequences set in advance. If there is no specific rule against throwing the cat through the plate glass window, when you hear the crash, you are faced with a flare-up situation.

I'm sure you will *not* take it calmly and say it doesn't matter, since windows are covered by insurance. (Are cats?) I'm sure you will *not* ask little Johnnie why he did it or ask him if the cat was being naughty to him. You will do neither of these calm, subdued things; in fact, if little Johnnie isn't careful, you may feel a strong urge—which you must resist—to send *him* through the window, too.

I would normally call it a key moment, but it's not one that you'll pay the least attention to. This is definitely a classic flare-up situation.

The keys to a flare-up are these:

—the incident requires some—usually immediate—disciplinary response

—there is generally a component of anger on your part

—and, most importantly, the incident was unanticipated.

The existence of anger means that your first response, for Johnnie's sake, should be to get him out of your sight. Put the charming little fellow in his room while you clean up the glass and patch up the cat. Then deal with Johnnie.

None of us likes flare-ups, but we all encounter them now and then.

II. PRE-SETS. Contrary to flare-ups, in the pre-set type of discipline, you've thought through the types of things that can happen in your house and have determined in advance the discipline that will apply to each infraction. While this may sound a little cold-blooded, it isn't.

THIS IS MERELY A WAY OF KEEPING YOUR EMOTIONS OUT OF AS MANY SITUATIONS AS POSSIBLE, FOR YOUR SAKE AND THE SAKE OF YOUR CHILDREN.

As many general categories as possible should be pre-planned in this way. An item that at the first infraction falls under the flare-up category can be moved to the pre-set type for the future.

There are three big advantages to pre-set discipline. After the first time or two a teenager comes in late, a rule about arrival time is set, and the accompanying discipline specified. Then, if the rule is broken again, there is no need for dad to be upset or to preach a fiery sermon—which keeps everyone up even later—about the evils of late hours. He merely applies the preset discipline. No accusations or arguments are necessary, and everyone is saved needless hostility. That's the first advantage to pre-sets.

The second is that, because consequences are planned in advance, the participative approach can be used. The teenager can have input into what the discipline for lateness ought to be. Then it's clear to everyone and the child can't accuse dad of unfairness or arbitrariness. He is merely the enforcer of the rules the family has predetermined, and the consequences are automatic.

The child knows he's broken the rule and he knows the consequences for it. He will expect nothing less than the discipline already pre-set. (Of course, as mentioned, there's always the possibility of a legitimate excuse. This is where dad can apply mercy if it's deserved. But in the absence of mitigating circumstances, the discipline is automatic.)

A third advantage to pre-sets is that they put more responsibility on the child to make his own choices, thereby removing the concept that this is a contest of wills. No longer is it child against dad. It's child against the rules that he had a part in making. He can "test" them if he wishes, but because he's helped make the rules, he knows he's testing the system, not the parents.

The pre-set approach removes dad and mom from the role of enforcer. This reminds me of one of the simplest ideas I ever heard for removing parents from the role of worrying, nail-biting, guilt-ridden disciplinarian. Instead of sitting up late waiting for a child to come in from a date, the parents set their alarm for a half hour after the teenager is to be home at night, thus making it *his* job to turn it off before it wakes up mom and dad.

The extra half-hour gives the child a reasonable leeway. If he doesn't make it, he's in trouble and knows he will receive the pre-set discipline—not because someone sat up worrying, getting angrier by the minute, but because the clock did its job.

We couldn't talk about discipline without commenting on an old question: to spank or not to spank. Most psychologists recommend against it; others feel it has its place in the raising of unruly children—young ones only—although even the advocates differentiate between a posterior swat with an open hand, and a beating, which is never acceptable.

Fitzhugh Dodson, a child psychologist, makes a good point in saying that, if you spank, do it—contrary to standard advice—when you're angry. It should be in the category of what I've called a flare-up, not a pre-set. Why? Because cold-blooded, non-angry spanking is the kind a child can't understand. Since, by the time it happens, he's probably nearly forgotten about the incident that caused the problem, or at least forgotten the depth of feeling engendered, he wonders how you can walk in and coolly whip him.

So if you're going to swat, do it when Johnnie throws the cat through the window, not the next morning after Jean Ann has sailed your record collection like frisbees out an upstairs window at passing cars.

You'll have to make your own decision about spankings, but keep two things in mind: first, they're for *your* good—not the good of the child; second, when you're spanking, you're also teaching—and what you're teaching is that bigger people are allowed to hit littler people.

Discipline, since it usually involves emotion on the part of parent and child, isn't an easy thing to be consistent in, even under pre-sets, but it's a vital part of raising a family. Take your role in it seriously, and tremble a little at the enormous power for excess that you hold.

Topics For Discussion With Your Wife

1. Do we have a system for the calmer parent to intercede and help the other calm down?
2. How do we feel about each of the points mentioned about discipline? Are there some we need to work on?
3. How can we move more of our discipline matters from flare-ups to pre-sets?
4. How do we feel about our discipline patterns in general? Are we being too strict, too lenient, or just right? Have we gotten into a pattern of being too harsh or too lenient with any one particular child?
5. How much in agreement are we on the ideas in this chapter? Are we working together? Have we identified areas of difference, and are we able to talk about them? Are there major areas we need to discuss further at a future time?

14

Don't be a Typical Dad

Someone has guessed that the typical American dad spends no more than two minutes a week in direct interaction with each of his children. This figure doesn't come from a research study so it may be inaccurate. But I'm afraid it's about right. Especially if you have several children in the house, give some thought to how much time you actually spent this past week with each one.

A typical dad isn't what we want to be. Of course, there's no such thing as a typical dad. We're all different in many ways. But I think there is a typical dad stereotype in America and that it contains these two components:

—dad leaves the "heavy" child-rearing to his wife;

—dad is a materialist, who believes that his only real contribution to the family is his income; he measures his worth as a man and a dad by the money he brings in and the quality of living he provides.

Fortunately, this is no longer an accurate stereotype for a great many dads. More and more, men are realizing that their families are their most important role in life and that fathers have more to offer than income.

HISTORICALLY, DADS HAVE PROVIDED AND MOTHERS HAVE NURTURED. BUT TODAY

PEOPLE KNOW THAT SUCH A SHARP DISTINCTION ISN'T THE IDEAL.

However, our upbringing by former-generation parents can interfere with our views of what could be today. As modern dads, we may agree, in principle, with the large role we can play in the lives of our children, yet when it comes to leaving the TV to change the baby, it will probably seem to be mom's job. We may not often have seen our own dads—who themselves were raised under different expectations—do such tasks as baby-changing, and that example carries the day. (I'm not saying that's necessarily bad; it depends on how both parties in the marriage view their roles.)

Some ideas die hard, as illustrated by a story of a ham. A groom was puzzled when his new bride cooked their first ham to see her cut off both ends before putting it in the oven. He asked her why she did it. The bride said her mother always cut off the ends, but she'd never asked her why. Later, the couple had dinner at the bride's parents. The groom asked his mother-in-law about the ham. Her answer was, "I don't know why I do that. My mother taught me."

The young man then called his wife's grandmother. "Why," he asked, "did you teach your daughter, who taught her daughter, to cut off the ends of a ham before cooking it?"

"Oh," the grandmother said, "I didn't teach my daughter that. She just must have observed it. I did that because my old-fashioned oven was too small for a whole ham."

So it is with much information we have about what a dad is. We've stored away certain ideas and images, and whether or not they make sense in today's world, we will probably carry them out unless we take the trouble to question them. We have to be more flexible than that to be good dads in the modern world.

To be better than "typical," here are some suggestions.

1. BE A GREAT HUSBAND. In a few years, you won't have any children at home. But you'll still have your wife at home. Stay close to her as you work together on this marvelous and wild adventure of raising kids. Let her grow and change, too. Listen to her, not just as you would a counselor, but as you would a full partner. Love her for herself, for what she does for your family, and, most of all, for

putting up with you.

Don't expect pampering. It might be nice for a dad to have wife, children, and dog meet him at the door every evening with slippers and newspaper, leading him to his easy chair and placing his feet on the hassock, then tiptoeing around because, "Daddy's had a hard day." A dad may get such treatment on Father's Day, at least while his children are small. But if that's part of a man's image of fatherhood, he'd better rid himself of that view right now. Be a liberated dad in a liberated family.

A man can't expect mind reading on the part of his wife or children either. Some couples get into difficulty because they assume that a loving spouse would say or do certain things, some of which the spouse had no idea about. Your wife will be from a different background and will have grown up under parents different from yours. Don't expect her to know just what you want all of the time. Talk, don't assume.

A few men have the view that, as heads of the house, they are kings. Forget it. The day of kings is past. You are partners with your wife in all things, including how you raise your children. (If I haven't mentioned that often enough in this book, it's because this is a book for dads.) If you prefer to see yourself as a king, keep in mind that kings are married to queens, not to scullery maids.

2. RE-CHANNEL YOUR ENERGIES. Many men work in an atmosphere of hard-driving competition. They feel they have great things to do in the world and have little time or energy for family matters. The secret is to re-channel a little of that great drive toward the family. It's just an attitude shift. Putting real energy and commitment into their children and wife is often more rewarding than anything they've ever done.

How many dads have felt cheated when they realized their sons and daughters grew up without them while they worked horrendous hours to become president of the bank? But surely there must have been moments at the bank when each of them knew that, if he dropped dead, business would go on as usual, after a two-hour closure for the funeral—and the audit.

"But it was all for the kids," these dads say.

"All we wanted was you," the children reply.

Write out your fatherhood goals just as you would other important goals in your life, such as career plans, and you'll find your family energies more focused. Share these goals with your wife. And then, ideally, share them with your children. Shared commitment is much more likely to produce results than mere private resolve.

3. RECOGNIZE THAT YOUR CHILDREN NEED YOU. Some dads say, "But being a parent today is too hard. Kids are too independent. They don't really need me. I'll just bring home the bacon and let them raise themselves. I don't understand their world." It's true that, in some ways, children are more independent these days at an earlier age. But if a dad thinks that means his kids don't need him, he hasn't been very observant.

I know it's been said that a parental "No" used to be an answer, whereas now it's a challenge—making it sound like the old days were better days to raise children. Well, I've always doubted that the good old days were quite as good as the selective memory of age tells people they were.

Clearly we live in a time when children grow up fast and have ideas of their own. While this causes our task to be difficult, none of us would go back to the "good old days" of smallpox, diphtheria, and whooping cough. These diseases and others claimed so many young children that some parents tried not to form deep attachments to their babies at first, so as to avoid some of the grief if they died of disease. I'll stick with the "good new days."

4. TRUST IN THE BASIC GOODNESS OF YOUTH. As to the big stuff, assume the basic goodness of your children unless you have specific reasons not to. It's easy to form the impression that young people are pretty rotten. More likely, if we knew their hearts, we would find most of them to be good people trying to be decent and to find their way in the world. If we will communicate to our children that we think of them that way, they will do better than if we are always suspicious, distrustful, and nosey.

5. OVERLOOK THE SMALL STUFF. A man once told me he was disturbed about a small dress and grooming matter in his twenty-two-year old son. I asked him if he had the same worry about his neighbor's son, and he said no.

"Then what does it really matter?" I asked.

"I guess it's just an image problem for me," he said. An honest answer. We can learn to tolerate the small stuff and rejoice in the uniqueness of individuals.

6. DON'T BE AFRAID TO INTERVENE. While we can value the unique qualities of each of our children, we also ought to consider intervening to help them change what might harm their chances in the world. The key is to intervene to "help," not to "demand" or "reject." A shy child can be helped to be more outgoing, for the sake of gaining confidence and making a more favorable impression. A child who doesn't do well in math needs help to keep from falling behind and to salvage his self-image.

Some parents take a *laissez-faire* attitude with their children's characteristics. But without demanding more than is reasonable, or insisting that the child conform to dad's way of doing things, a dad can help his child improve in areas where, without improvement, his chances for success in society would be weakened. Often, without this intervention, the child would have no idea how he comes across. Maybe his best friend wouldn't tell him, but his father should.

By the time they're teenagers, youth can be left to make the final decision about many of these matters, but they should be offered the chance to improve and change.

7. BE BETTER THAN YOUR OWN DAD. I heard a man say that while he loved his own dad and greatly respected the job he had done, his own goal was to be an even better dad. Each generation should do a better job as parents. We have more resources, information, and time to devote to the task than any other generation in history. Make it your goal to be better at the job than your dad was—even if he was great.

To do that, you'll have to grow and develop as a person, just as you expect such growth from your children. Some of us hide behind personal weaknesses. "I've always had a bad temper," some people say, as if they were telling the color of their eyes, the shape of their nose, or other characteristics they couldn't change. A bad temper can be changed. So can other character faults. No one ought to hide behind a argument like, "That's just the way I am." Now that the dragon has been identified, we must pick up whatever weapon we can find and kill it.

"I do my best," is another poor response some people give. It implies that a complaint about their performance is unfair, that they've valiantly done all that could be done. When Paul was approached by his wife about showing more interest in schoolwork and other projects in which his children were involved, he flubbed his key moment at first. He snapped, "I do the best I can with the time I have."

Paul took his wife's comment as an accusation that he was a poor dad, rather than as a suggestion to take extra time with his children. When he finally settled down and listened, he discovered that his wife had a point. With minimal reorganization of his evening hours, he provided his children with better access to him.

Don't ever say, "I do my best." Say, "What did you have in mind?"

WITH ALL THE EXPECTATIONS WE HAVE FOR OUR CHILDREN'S GROWTH AND DEVELOPMENT, A DAD HAS TO GROW, TOO.

Your teenagers will probably claim, at some point, that their younger siblings were raised differently from what they were. Partly that is their biased memory. But, partly, I hope it's true. You should be a better parent after being broken in than you were at the start, shouldn't you?

We expect improvement in all other area of our lives. Most salaried jobs provide raises every year, premised on the idea that another year of experience has made us better employees. That should be true of parenting, too—though we probably won't get the raise.

We also have to be aware of what accusations such as "You didn't buy me as many things as you buy Bobby," really might mean. When your teenager tells you his little brother has it easier than he had it, consider that what he might be meaning is, "You love him more than you loved me." Listen to what he says and try to figure out what he means. Take a breath, tell him you will think about what he's said and get back to him. Then, think about it and get back to him.

We have to be flexible and always growing to deal with the specific and varying needs of our children. The job really doesn't get any easier because each child is different and that's part of what causes those inevitable conflicts. It's also what adds spice and joy to the job.

The more integrated and at peace we are as individuals, the better we are at everything we do, including fatherhood. But just as our children need time to develop, so do we. Patience with ourselves in vital since there are no quick fixes for becoming better people.

You know by now that I think your greatest accomplishments in life will be with your family. Make fatherhood fun, make it worth spending energy and time on. Give it your best, and don't ever give up. Certainly you mustn't think of it as too big a job for you. While it's a job with the greatest possible challenges, it also has the greatest potential for success. It's a job a "regular dad" can do.

Index

A

Abuse, 149.

Acceptance
　teaching children to
　　accept life, 84.
　teaching children to accept
　　themselves, 130-131.

Achievement, feeling of,
　through work, 70.

Acknowledgment, of conflicts, 158.

Adult, at eighteen, 112-113.

Advice, for mothers, valuable
　for fathers, 21.

Allowance, 76-77.

Anger, how to handle, 149-151.

Approval, don't withhold, 34-35.

Awareness, of father's role, 22.

B

Bribes, 75.

C

Caring, 158.

Children
　their need for dad's
　　influence, 166.
　their view of dad, 20.

Chastisement, 28.

Choices, see Decisions.

Chore Chart, 72-73.

Compensators, 85.

Competition
　between siblings, 134-135.
　life not a, 85, 125.

Compliments, 35, 41.

Compromise, 154-155.

Conflicting needs, 142.

Conflicts, parent-child
　categorize, 157.

handle, not hide, 30.

Conformity, 97-98.

Consequences, as form of
　discipline, 152.

Conversation, see Talking.

Coping Skills, 84-85.

Creators, of fatherhood, 19-22.

D

Dad
　central to child rearing, 21.
　needs to become a
　　better person, 167-169.
　needs to love, 32-33.

Decision-making
　acceptance by parents
　　of kids', 109-111.
　requires practice, 103-106.

Demands, see Pressures.

Difficulties, cause growth, 108-109.

Discipline
　flare-ups, 159-160.
　match to infraction, 155-156.
　natural consequences, 152.
　not ownership, 152-153.
　not excessive, 153-154.
　pre-sets, 160-161.
　with love, 29, 151-152.

E

Effort, required to be a dad, 21.

Energy, 165-166.

Equality
　with children, 62.
　teaching it, 130-131, 137.

Example, 117.

F

G

H

I

K

L

M

N

O